**Lighted to Lighten: The Hope of India,
a Study of Conditions among Women in India**

INTRODUCTION

To say that the world is one is to-day's commonplace. What causes its new solidarity? What but the countless hands that reach across its shores and its Seven Seas, hands that devastate and hands that heal! There are the long fingers of the cable and telegraph that pry through earth's hidden places, gathering choice bits of international gossip and handing them out to all the breakfast tables of the Great Neighborhood. There are the swift fingers of transcontinental train and ocean liner, pushing the dweller from the West into the Far East, the man from the prairie into the desert. There are the devastating fingers of war that first fashion and then carry infernal machines and spread them broadcast over towns and ships and fertile fields. Thank God, there are also hands of kindness that dispense healing medicines, that scatter schoolbooks among untaught children and the Word of God in all parts of earth's neighborhood. And, lastly, there are hands that seem never to leave the house roof and the village street, yet gain the power of the long reach and set thousands of candles alight across the world.

"Why don't you let them alone? Their religion is good enough for them," was the classic comment of the armchair critic of a generation ago. Time has answered it. Nothing in to-day's world ever lets anything else alone. We read the morning paper in terms of continents. To the League of Nations China and Chile are concerns as intimate as Upper Silesia. To the Third Internationale the obscure passes of Afghanistan are a near frontier. Suffrage and prohibition are echoed in the streets of Poona and in the councils of Delhi. Labor strikes in West Virginia and Wales produce reactions in the cotton mills of Madras. And the American girl in high school, in college, in business, in society, in a profession, is producing her double under tropic suns, in far-off streets where speech and dress and manners are strange, but the heart of life is one. That time is past; we cannot let them alone; we can only choose what shall be the shape and fashioning done by hands that reach across the sea.

CHAPTER ONE

YESTERDAY AND TO-DAY

"Once upon a Time."

"Once upon a time,"[1] men and women dwelt in caves and cliffs and fashioned curious implements from the stones of the earth and painted crude pictures upon the walls of their rock dwellings. Archaeologists find such traces in England and along the river valleys of France, among the sands of Egyptian deserts and in India, where armor heads, ancient pottery, and cromlechs mark the passing of a long forgotten race. Thus India claims her place in the universal childhood of the world.

The Brown-skinned Tribes.

"Once upon a time,"[2] when the Stone Men had passed, a strange, new civilization is thought to have girdled the earth, passing probably in a "brown belt" from Mediterranean lands across India to the Pacific world and the Americas. Its sign was the curious symbol of the Swastika; its passwords certain primitive customs common to all these lands. Its probable Indian representatives are known to-day as Dravidians—the brown-skinned people still dominating South Indian life, whose exact place in the family of races puzzles every anthropologist. It was then that civilization was first walking up and down the great river valleys of the Old World. While the first pyramids[3] were a-building beside the long green ribbon of the Nile and the star-gazers[4] of Mesopotamia were reading future events from her towers of sun-dried bricks, Dravidian tribes were cultivating the rich mud of the Ganges valley, a slow-changing race. Did the lonely traveler, I wonder, troll the same air then as now to ward away evil spirits from the star-lit road? Did the Dravidian maiden do her sleek hair in the same knot at the nape of her brown neck, and poise the earthen pot with the same grace on her daily pilgrimage to the river?

The Aryan Brother.

"Once upon a time" Abraham pitched his tent beneath the oaks of Mamre, and Moses shepherded his father-in-law's flocks at "the back side of the desert." It was then that down through the grim passes of the Himalayas, where now the British regiments convoy caravans and guard the outposts of Empire, a people of fair skin and strange speech migrated southward to the Land of the Five Rivers and the fat plains of the Ganges. Aryan even as we, the Brahman entered India, singing hymns to the sun and the dawn, bringing with him the stately Sanskrit speech, new lore of priest and shrine, new pride of race that was to cleave society into those horizontal strata that persist to-day in the caste system. Thus through successions of Stone-Age men, Dravidian tribes, and Aryan invaders, India stretches her roots deep into the past. But while there were transpiring these

"Old, unhappy, far-off things
And battles long ago,"

where were we? The superior Anglo-Saxon who speaks complacently of "the native" forgets that during that same "once upon a time" when civilization was old in India, his ancestors, clad in deer skin and blue paint, were stalking the forests of Europe for food.

Gifts to the West.

Nor did these old civilizations forbear to reach hands across the sea and share with the young and lusty West the fruits of their knowledge. On a May morning, as skillful carriers swing you up to the heights of the South India hills, there is a sudden sound reminiscent of the home barnyard, a scurry of wings across the path, and a gleam of glossy plumage; Mr. Jungle Cock has been disturbed in his morning meal. Did you know that from his ancestors are descended in direct lineage all the Plymouth Rocks and the White Leghorns of the poultry yard, all the Buff Orpingtons that win gold medals at poultry shows? Other food stuffs India originated and shared.

Sugar and rice were delicacies from her fields carried over Roman roads to please the palates of the Caesars.[5]

Traditions of Womanhood.

Besides these contributions to the world's pantry, there were gifts of the mind and spirit. To those days of long ago modern India looks back as to a golden age, for she was then in the forefront of civilization, passing out her gifts with a generous hand. Of that ancient heritage not the least part is the tradition of womanhood,—a heritage trampled in the dust of later ages, its restoration only now beginning through that liberty in Christ which sets free the woman of the West and of the East.

Much might be written on the place of the Indian woman in folk-lore epic and drama. Helen of Troy and Dido of Carthage pale into common adventuresses when placed beside the quiet courage and utter self-abnegation of such Indian heroines as Sita and Damayanti.

The story of Rama and Sita is the Odyssey of the East, crooned by grandmothers over the evening fires; sung by wandering minstrels under the shade of the mango grove; trolled by travelers jogging in bullock carts along empty moonlit roads. Sita's devotion is a household word to many a woman-child of India. Little Lakshmi follows the adventures of the loved heroine as she shares Rama's unselfish renunciation of the throne and exile to the forest with its alarms of wild beasts and wild men. She thrills with fear at Sita's abduction by the hideous giant, Ravana, and the wild journey through the air and across the sea to the Ceylon castle. She weeps with Rama's despair, and again laughs with glee at the antics of his monkey army from the south country, as they build their bridge of stones across the Ceylon straits where now-a-days British engineers have followed in their simian track and train and ferry carry the casual traveler across the gaps jumped by the monkey king and his tribe. Sita's sore temptations in the palace of her conqueror and her steadfast loyalty until at last her husband comes victorious—they are part of the heritage of a million Lakshmis all up and down the length of India.

[Illustration: WHAT WILL LIFE BRING TO HER?]

Of the loves of Nala and Damayanti it is difficult to write in few words. From the opening scene where the golden-winged swans carry Nala's words of love to Damayanti in the garden, sporting at sunset with her maidens, the old tale moves on with beauty and with pathos. The Swayamvara, or Self Choice, harks back to the time when the Indian princess might herself choose among her suitors. Gods and men compete for Damayanti's hand among scenes as bright and stately as the lists of King Arthur's Court, until the princess, choosing her human lover, throws about his neck the garland that declares her choice. Happy years follow, and the birth of children. Then the scene changes to exile and desertion. Through it all moves the heroine, sharing her one garment with her unworthy lord, "thin and pale and travel-stained, with hair covered in dust," yet never faltering until her husband, sane and repentant, is restored to home and children and throne.

So the ancient folk-lore goes on, in epic and in drama, with the woman ever the heroine of the tale. True it is that her virtues are limited; obedience, chastity, and an unlimited capacity for suffering largely sum them up. They would scarcely satisfy the ambitions of the new woman of to-day; yet some among us might do well to pay them reverence.

Those were the high days of Indian womanhood. Then, as the centuries passed, there came slow eclipse. Lawgivers like Manu[6] proclaimed the essential impurity of a woman's heart; codes and customs began to bind her with chains easy to forge and hard to break. Later followed the catastrophe that completed the change. The Himalayan gateways opened once more and through them swarmed a new race of invaders, passing out of those barren plains of Central Asia that have been ever the breeding grounds of nations and swooping upon India's treasures. In one hand the green flag of the Prophet, in the other the sword, these followers of Muhammad sealed for a millennium the end of woman's high estate.

All was not lost without a mighty struggle.[7] From those days come the tales of Rajput chivalry—tales that might have been sung by the troubadours of France. Rajput maidens of noble blood scorned the throne of Muslim conquerors. Litters supposed to carry captive women poured out warriors armed to the teeth. Men and women in saffron robes and bridal garments mounted the great funeral pyre, and when the conquering Allah-ud-din entered the silent city of Chitore he found no resistance and no captives, for no one living was left from the great Sacrifice of Honorable Death.

After that came an end. Everywhere the Muhammadan conqueror desired many wives; in a far and alien land his own womankind were few. Again and again the ordinary Hindu householder, lacking the desperate courage of the Rajput, stood by helpless, like the Armenian of to-day, while his wife and daughter were carried off from before his eyes, to increase the harem of his ruler. Small wonder that seclusion became the order of the day—a woman would better spend her life behind the purdah of her own home than be added to the zenana of her conqueror. Later when the throes of conquest were over and Hindu women once more ventured forth to a wedding or a festival, small wonder that they copied the manners of their masters, and to escape familiarity and insult became as like as possible to women of the conquering race. Thus the use of the veil began.

At that beginning we do not wonder; what makes us marvel is that a repressing custom became so strong that, even after a century and a half of

British rule, all over North India and among some conservative families of the South seclusion and the veil still persist. Walk the streets of a great commercial town like Calcutta, and you find it a city of men. An occasional Parsee lady, now and then an Indian Christian, here and there women of the cooly class whose lowly station has saved their freedom—otherwise womankind seems not to exist.

The high hour of Indian womanhood had passed, not to return until brought back by the power of Christ, in whose kingdom there is "neither male nor female, but all are one." Yet as the afterglow flames up with a transient glory after the swift sunset, so in the gathering darkness of Muhammadan domination we see the brightness of two remarkable women.

There was Nur Jahan, the "Light of the World," wife of the dissolute Jahangir. Never forgetful, it would seem, of a childish adventure when the little Nur Jahan in temper and pride set free his two pet doves, twenty years later the Mughal Emperor won her from her soldier husband by those same swift methods that David employed to gain the wife of Uriah, the Hittite.

And when Nur Jahan became queen she was ruler indeed, "the one overmastering influence in his life."[8] From that time on we see her, restraining her husband from his self-indulgent habits, improving his administration, crossing flooded rivers and leading attacks on elephants to save him from captivity; "a beautiful queen, beautifully dressed, clever beyond compare, contriving and scheming, plotting, planning, shielding and saving, doing all things for the man hidden in the pampered, drink-sodden carcass of the king; the man who, for her at any rate, always had a heart." Think of Nur Jahan's descendants, hidden in the zenanas of India. When their powers, age-repressed, are set free by Christian education, what will it mean for the future of their nation?

[Illustration: MEENACHI OF MADURA
The Average Girl, a Bride at Twelve]

Then there came the lady of the Taj, Mumtaz Mahal, beloved of Shah Jahan, the Master Builder. We know less of her history, less of the secret of her charm, only that she died in giving birth to her thirteenth child, and that for all those years of married life she had held her husband's adoration. For twenty-two succeeding years he spent his leisure in collecting precious things from every part of his world that there might be lacking no adornment to the most exquisite tomb ever raised. And when it was finished —rare commentary on the contradiction of Mughal character—the architect was blinded that he might never produce its like again.

All that was a part of yesterday—a story of rise and fall; of woman's repression, with outbursts of greatness; of countless treasures of talent and possibilities unrecognized and undeveloped, hidden behind the doors of Indian zenanas. What of to-day?

TO-DAY: The Average Girl.

Meenachi of Madura, if she could become articulate, might tell us something of the life of the average girl to-day. Being average, she belongs neither to the exclusive streets of the Brahman, nor to the hovels of the untouchable outcastes, but to the area of the great middle class which is in India as everywhere the backbone of society. Meenachi's father is a weaver of the far-famed Madura muslins with their gold thread border. Her earliest childhood memory is the quiet weavers' street where the afternoon sun glints under the tamarind trees and, striking the long looms set in the open air, brings out the blue and mauve, the deep crimson and purple and gold of the weaving.

There were rollicking babyhood days when Meenachi, clad only in the olive of her satin skin with a silver fig leaf and a bead necklace for adornment, wandered in and out the house and about the looms at will. With added years came the burden of clothing, much resented by the wearer, but accepted with philosophic submission, as harder things would be later on. Toys are few and simple. The palmyra rattle is exchanged for the stiff wooden doll, painted in gaudy colors, and the collection of tiny vessels in which sand and stones and seeds provide the equivalent of mud pies in repasts of imaginary rice and curry. Household duties begin also. Meenachi at the age of six grasps her small bundle of broom-grass and sweeps each morning her allotted section of verandah. Soon she is helping to polish the brass cooking pots and to follow her mother and older sisters, earthen waterpot on hip, on their morning and evening pilgrimages to the river.

Being only an average girl, Meenachi will never go to school. There are ninety and nine of these "average" unschooled girls to the one "above the average" to whom education offers its outlet for the questing spirit. She looks with curiosity at the books her brother brings home from high school, but the strange, black marks which cover their pages mean nothing to her. Not for her the release into broad spaces that comes only through the written word. For, mark you, to the illiterate life means only those circumscribed experiences that come within the range of one's own sight and touch and hearing. "What I have seen, what I have heard, what I have felt"—there experience ends. From personal unhappiness there is no escape into the world current.

Meenachi is twelve and the freedom of the long street is hers no more. Yellow chrysanthemums in her glossy hair, a special diet of milk and curds and sweet cakes fried in ghee, and the outspoken congratulations of relatives, male and female, mark her entrance into the estate of womanhood. What the West hides, the East delights to reveal.

Now follows the swift sequel of marriage. The husband, of just the right degree of relationship, has long been chosen. The family exchequer is drained to the dregs to provide the heavy dowry, the burdensome expenditure for wedding feast and jewels, and the presentation of numerous wedding garments to equally numerous and expectant relatives. Meenachi is carried away by the splendor of new clothes and jewels and processions, and the general *tamash* of the occasion. Has she not the handsomest bridegroom and the most expensive *trousseau,* of this marriage month? Is she not the envy of all her former playmates? Only now and then comes a strange feeling of loneliness when she thinks of leaving the dear, familiar roof the narrow street with its tamarind trees and many colored looms. The mother-in-law's house is a hundred miles away, and the mother-in-law's face is strange.

Will Meenachi be sad or happy? The answer is complex and hard to find, for it depends on many contingencies. The husband—what will he be? He is not of Meenachi's choosing. Did she choose her father and mother, and the house in which she was born? Were they not chosen for her, "written upon her forehead" by her *Karma,* her inscrutable fate? Her husband has been chosen; let her make the best of the choice.

Will she be happy? The future years shall make answer by many things. Will she bear sons to her husband? If so, will her young body have strength for the pains of childbirth and the torturings of ignorant and brutal midwives? Will her *Karma* spare to her the life of husband and children? In India sudden death is never far; pestilence walks in darkness and destruction wastes at noon day. The fear of disease, the fear of demons, the fear of death will be never far away; for these fears there will be none to say, "Be not afraid."

So Meenachi, the bride, passes out into the unknown of life, and later into the greater unknown of death. No one has taught her to say in the valley of the shadow, "I will fear no evil, for Thou art with me." The terrors of life are with her, but its consolations are not hers.

[Illustration: MARRIED TO THE GOD
A Little Temple Girl]

Widowhood.

Of widowhood I shall say little. Since the ancient days of *suttee* when the wife mounted her husband's funeral pyre volumes have been written on the lot of the Indian widow. To-day in some cases the power of Christianity has awakened the spirit of social reform and the rigors of widowhood are lessened. Among the majority the old remains. In general, the higher you rise in the social scale, the sterner the conventions and fashions of widowhood become.

In Madras you may visit a Widow's Home, where through the wise efforts of a large-hearted woman in the Educational Department of Government more than a hundred Brahman girl-widows live the life of a normal schoolgirl. No fastings, no shaven heads, no lack of pretty clothes or jewels mark them off from the rest of womanhood. Schools and colleges open their doors and professional life as teacher or doctor offers hope of human contact and interest for these to whom husband and child and home are forever forbidden. In all India you may find a very few such institutions, but "what are these among so many?" The millions of repressed child widows still go on.

Wives of the Idol.

Worse is the fate of those whose *Karma* condemns them to a life of religious prostitution. Perhaps the first-born son of the family lies near to death. The parents vow a frantic vow to the deity of the local temple. "Save our son's life, O Govinda; our youngest daughter shall be dedicated to thy service." The son recovers, the vow must be fulfilled, and bright-eyed, laughing Lakshmi, aged eight, is led to the temple, put through the mockery of a ceremony of marriage to the black and misshapen image in the inmost shrine, and thenceforth trained to a religious service of nameless infamy.

The story of Hinduism holds the history of some devout seekers after God, of sincere aspiration, in some cases of beautiful thought and life. This deepest blot is acknowledged and condemned by its better members. Yet in countless temples, under the brightness of the Indian sun, the iniquity, protected by vested interests, goes on and no hand is lifted to stay. Suppose each American church to shelter its own house of prostitution, its forces recruited from the young girls of the congregation, their services at the disposal of its worshippers. The thought is too black for utterance; yet just so in the life of India has the service of the gods been prostituted to the lusts of men.

Reform.

The achievements of Christianity in India are not confined to the four million who constitute the community that have followed the new Way. Perhaps even greater has been the reaction it has excited in the ranks of Hinduism among those who would repudiate the name of Christian. Chief among the abuses of Hinduism to be attacked has been the traditional attitude toward woman. Child marriage and compulsory widowhood are condemned by every social reformer up and down the length of India. The battle is fought not only for women, but by them also. Agitation for the suffrage has been carried on in India's chief cities. In Poona not long since the educated women of the city, Hindu, Muhammadan, and Christian, joined in a procession with banners, demanding compulsory education for girls.

Of women not Christian, but freed from ancient bonds by this reflex action of Christian thought, perhaps the most eminent example is Mrs. Sarojini Naidu. Of Brahman birth, but English education, she dared to resist the will of her family and the tradition of her caste and marry a man of less than Brahman extraction. Now as a writer of distinction second only to Tagore she is known to Europe as well as to India. In her own country she is perhaps loved best for her intense patriotism, and is the best known woman connected with the National Movement.

Chiefly, however, it is among the Christian community that woman's freedom has become a fact. Women such as Mrs. Naidu exist, but they are few. Now and then one reads of a case of widow-remarriage successfully achieved. Too often, however, the Hindu reformer, however well-meaning and sincere, talks out his reformation in words rather than deeds. He lacks the support of Christian public opinion; he lacks also the vitalizing power of a personal Christian experience. It is easy to speak in public on the evils of early marriage; he speaks and the audience applauds. He knows too well that in the applauding audience there is not a man whose son will marry his daughter if she passes the age of twelve. So the ardent reformer talks on, with the abandon of the darky preacher who exhorted his audience "Do as I say and not as I do"; and hopes that in some future incarnation life will be kinder, and he may be able to carry out the excellent practices he really desires.

A Hindu girl of high family was allowed to go to college. There being then no women's college in her part of India, she entered a Government University in a large city, where there were a few other women students.

Western standards of freedom prevailed and were accepted by men and women. Rukkubai shared in social as well as academic life. With a strong arm and a steady eye, she distinguished herself at tennis and badminton, and came even to play in mixed doubles, a mark of the most "advanced" social views to be found in India.

After college came marriage to a man connected with the family of a well known rajah. The husband was not only the holder of a University degree similar to her own, but a zealous social reformer, eloquent in his advocacy of women's freedom. Life promised well for Rukkubai. A year or two later a friend visited her behind the purdah, with the doors of the world shut in her face. The zeal of the reforming husband could not stand against the petty persecutions of the older women of the family. "I wish," said Rukkubai, "that I had never known freedom. Now I have known—and lost."

[Illustration: WILL LIFE BE KIND TO HER?]

Yet not all reformers are such. There are an increasing number whose deeds keep pace with their words. Such may be found among the members of The Servants of India Society, who spend part of the year in social studies; the remainder in carrying to ignorant people the message they have learned.

Such is the heritage of the Hindu woman of ancient freedom; centuries when traditions of repression have gripped with ever-tightening hold; to-day a new ferment in the blood, a new striving toward purposes half realized.

Of to-morrow, who can say? The future is hidden, but the chapters that follow may perhaps serve to bring us into touch with a few of the many forces that are helping to shape the day that shall be.

[Footnote 1: History of India, E.W. Thompson. Christian Literature Society, London and Madras, pp. 11-12.]

[Footnote 2: Outline of History, H.G. Wells. Vol. I, pp. 146-8.]

[Footnote 3: Outline of History, H.G. Wells, Vol. I, pp. 196-199.]

[Footnote 4: Outline of History, H.G. Wells, Vol. I, pp. 189-190.]

[Footnote 5: Ancient Times, Breasted, pp. 658-9.]

[Footnote 6: Code of Manu, Book 9, quoted Lux Christi, Mason, p. 14.]

[Footnote 7: India through the Ages, Florence Annie Steele, Routledge, pp. 95-104, 116-18.]

[Footnote 8: India through the Ages, pp. 190-200]

CHAPTER TWO

AT SCHOOL

Hindu or Christian.

In the last chapter we have spoken of the Hindu girl as yet untouched by Christianity, save as such influence may have filtered through into the general life of the nation. We have had vague glimpses of her social inheritance, with its traditions of an ancient and honorable estate of womanhood; of the limitations of her life to-day; of her half-formed aspirations for the future.

Of education as such nothing has been said. As we turn now from home to school life, we shall turn also from the Hindu community to the Christian. This does not mean that none but Christian girls go to school. In all the larger and more advanced cities and in some towns you will find Government schools for Hindu girls as well as those carried on by private enterprise, some of them of great efficiency. Yet this deliberate turning to the school life of the Christian community is not so arbitrary as it seems.

In the first place, the proportion of literacy among Christian women is far higher than among the Hindu and Muhammadan communities. Again, because a large proportion of Christians have come from the depressed classes, the "submerged tenth," ground for uncounted centuries under the heel of the caste system, their education is also a study in social uplift, one of the biggest sociological laboratory experiments to be found anywhere on earth. And, lastly, it is through Christian schools that the girls and women of America have reached out hands across the sea and gripped their sisters of the East.

The School under the Palm Trees.

"And the dawn comes up like thunder Outer China 'cross the Bay." Far from China and far inland from the Bay is this South Indian village, but the dawn flashes up with the same amazing swiftness. Life's daily resurrection proceeds rapidly in the Village of the Seven Palms. Flocks of crows are swarming in from their roosting place in the palmyra jungle beside the dry sand river; the cattle are strolling out from behind various enclosures where they share the family shelter; all around is the whirr of bird and insect as the teeming life of the tropics wakes to greet "my lord Sun."

Under the thatch of each mud-walled hovel of the outcaste village there is the same stir of the returning day. Sheeted corpses stretched on the floor suddenly come to life and the babel of village gossip begins.

In the house at the far end of the street, Arul is first on her feet, first to rub the sleep from her eyes. There is no ceremony of dressing, no privacy in which to conduct it if there were. Arul rises in the same scant garment in which she slept, snatches up the pot of unglazed clay that stands beside the door, poises it lightly on her hip, and runs singing to the village well, where each house has its representative waiting for the morning supply. There is the plash of dripping water, the creak of wheel and straining rope, and the chatter of girl voices.

[Illustration: A TEMPLE IN SOUTH INDIA]

The well is also the place for making one's morning toilet. Arul dashes the cold water over her face, hands, and feet. No soap is required, no towel —the sun is shining and will soon dry everything in sight. Next comes the tooth-brushing act, when a smooth stick takes the place of a brush, and "Kolynos" or "Colgate" is replaced by a dab of powdered charcoal. Arul combs her hair only for life's great events, such as a wedding or a festival, and changes her clothes so seldom that it is better form not to mention it.

Breakfast is equally simple,—and the "simple life" at close range is apt to lose many of its charms. In the corner of the one windowless room that serves for all domestic purposes stands the earthen pot of black gruel. It is made from the *ragi*, little, hard, round seeds that resemble more than anything else the rape seed fed to a canary. It looks a sufficiently unappetizing breakfast, but contentment abounds because the pot is full, and that happens only when rains are abundant and seasons prosperous. The Russian peasant and his black bread, the Indian peasant and his black gruel —dark symbols these of the world's hunger line.

There is no sitting down to share even this simple meal, no conception of eating as a social event, a family sacrament. The father, as lord and master, must be served first; then the children seize the one or two cups by turn, and last of all comes Mother. Arul gulps her breakfast standing and then dashes into the street. She is one of the village herd girls; the sun is up and shining hot, and the cattle and goats are jostling one another in their impatience to be off for the day.

The dry season is on and all the upland pastures are scorched and brown. A mile away is the empty bed of the great tank. A South Indian tank in our parlance would be an artificial lake. A strong earth wall, planted with palmyras, encircles its lower slope. The upper lies open to receive surface water, as well as the channel for the river that runs full during the monsoon months. During the "rains" the country is full of water, blue and sparkling. Now the water is gone, the crops are ripening, and in the clay tank bottom the cattle spend their days searching for the last blades of grass.

"Watch the cows well, Little Brother," calls Arul, as she hurries back on the narrow path that winds between boulders and thickets of prickly pear cactus. Green parrots are screaming in the tamarind trees and overhead a white-throated Brahmany kite wheels motionless in the vivid blue. The sun is blazing now, but Arul runs unheeding. It is time for school—she knows it by the sun-clock in the sky. "Female education," as the Indian loves to call it, is not yet fashionable in the Village of the Seven Palms. With twenty-five boys there are only three girls who frequent its halls of learning. Of the three Arul is one. Her father, lately baptized, knows but little of what Christ's religion means, but the few facts he has grasped are written deeply in his simple mind and show life-results. One of these ideas is that the way out and up is through the gate of Christian education. And so it is that Arul comes to school. She is but eight, yet with a mouth to feed and a body to clothe, and the rice pot often empty, the halving of her daily wage means self-denial to all the family. So it is that Arul, instead of herding cattle all day, runs swiftly back to the one-roomed schoolhouse under the cocoanuts and arrives not more than half an hour late.

The schoolroom is so primitive that you would hardly recognize it as such. Light and air and space are all too little. There are no desks or even benches. A small, wooden blackboard and the teacher's table and rickety chair are all that it can boast in the way of equipment. The only interesting thing in sight is the children themselves, rows of them on the floor, writing letters in the sand. Unwashed they are, uncombed and almost unclothed, but with all the witchery of childhood in their eyes. In that bare room lies the possibility of transforming the life of the Village of the Seven Palms.

But the teacher is innocent of the ways of modern pedagogy, and deep and complicated are the snares of the Tamil alphabet with its two hundred and sixteen elusive characters. Baffling, too, are the mysteries of number combination. "If six mangoes cost three annas, how much will one mango cost?" Arul never had an anna of her own, how should she know? The teachers bamboo falls on her hard, little hand, and two hot tears run down and drop on the cracked slate. The way to learning is long and beset with as many thorns as the crooked path through the prickly pear cactus. Bible stories are happier. Arul can tell you how the Shepherds sang and all about the little boy who gave his own rice cakes and dried fish, to help Jesus feed hungry people. She has been hungry so often that that story seems real.

The years pass over Arul's head, leaving her a little taller, a little fleeter of foot as she hurries back from the pasture, a little wiser in the ways of God and men. Still her father holds out against the inducements of child labor. Arul shall go to school as long as there is anything left for her to learn. And into Arul's eyes there has come the gleam of a great ambition. She will leave the Village of the Seven Palms and go into the wide world.

The most spacious existence she knows of is represented by the Girls' Boarding School in the town twenty miles away. To enter that school, to study, to become a teacher perhaps—but beyond that the wings of Arul's imagination have not yet learned to soar. The meaning of service for Christ and India, the opportunity of educated womanhood, such ideas have not yet entered Arul's vocabulary. She will learn them in the days to come.

Countless villages of the Seven Palms; countless schools badly equipped and poorly taught; countless Aruls—feeling within them dim gropings, half-formed ambitions. Somewhere in America there are girls trained in rural education and longing for the chance for research and original work in a big, untried field. What a chance for getting together the girl and the task!

[Illustration: THE SORT OF HOME THAT ARUL KNEW IN THE VILLAGE OF SEVEN PALMS]

A HIGH SCHOOL

Where the Girls Come from.

If the girls of India could pass you in long procession, you would need to count up to one hundred before you found one who had had Arul's opportunity of learning just to read and write. Infinitely smaller is the proportion of those who go into secondary schools. American women have been responsible for founding, financing, and teaching many of the Girls' High Schools that exist. They are of various sorts. Some have new and up-to-date plants, modelled on satisfactory types of American buildings. Others are muddling along with old-time, out-grown schoolrooms, spilling over into thatched sheds, and longing for the day when the spiritual structure they are erecting will be expressed in a suitable material form. Schools vary also as to social standing, discipline, and ideals; yet there are common features and problems, and one may be more or less typical of all. Most include under one organization everything from kindergarten to senior high school, so that the school is really a big family of one or two or four hundred, as the case may be.

The girls come from many grades of Indian life. The great majority are Christians, for few Hindu parents are yet sufficiently "advanced" to desire a high school education for their daughters, and those who do usually send their girls to a Government school where caste regulations will be observed and where there will be no religious teaching.

Some of the Christian girls come from origins as crude as that of Arul. To such the simplest elements of hygiene are unknown, and cleanly and decent living is the first and hardest lesson to be learned. Others are orphans, waifs, and strays cast up from the currents of village life. Uncared for, undernourished, with memories of a tragic childhood behind them, it is sometimes an impossible task to turn these little, old women back into normal children. But the largest number are children of teachers and catechists, pastors, and even college professors, who come from middle class homes, with a greater or less collection of Christian habits and ideals. With all these is a small scattering of high caste Hindu girls, the children of exceptionally liberal parents. The resulting school community is a wonderful example of pure democracy. Ignorant village girls learn more from the "public opinion" of their better trained schoolmates than from any amount of formal discipline; while daughters of educated families share their inheritance and come to realize a little of the need of India's illiterate masses. So school life becomes an experiment in Christian democracy, where a girl counts only for what she can do and be; where each member contributes something to the life of the group and receives something from it.

What the Girls Study.

Schools are schools the world over, and the agonies of the three R's are common to children in whatever tongue they learn. An Indian kindergarten is not so different from an American, except for language and local color. Equipment is far simpler and less expensive, but there is the same spontaneity, the same joy of living; laughter and play have the same sound in Tamil as in English. Besides, Indian kindergartens produce some charming materials all their own—shiny black tamarind seeds, piles of colored rice, and palm leaves that braid into baby rattles and fans.

So, too, a high school course is much the same even in India. The right-angled triangle still has an hypotenuse, and quadratics do not simplify with distance, while Tamil classics throw Vergil and Cicero into the shade. The fact that high school work is all carried on in English is the biggest stumbling block in the Indian schoolgirl's road to learning. What would the American girl think of going through a history recitation in Russian, writing chemistry equations in French, or demonstrating a geometry proposition in Spanish? Some day Indian education may be conducted in its own vernaculars; to-day there are neither the necessary text-books, nor the vocabulary to express scientific thought. As yet, and probably for many years to come, the English language is the key that unlocks the House of Learning to the schoolgirl. Indian classics she has and they are well worth knowing; but even Shakespeare and Milton would hardly console the American girl for the loss of all her story books, from "Little Women" and "Pollyanna" up—or down—to the modern novel. To understand English sufficiently to write and speak and even think in it is the big job of the High School. It is only the picked few who attain unto it; those few are possessed of brains and perseverance enough to become the leaders of the next generation.

School Life.

It is not unusual for an Indian girl to spend ten or twelve years in such a boarding school. An institution is a poor substitute for a home, but in such cases it must do its best to combine the two. This means that books are almost accessories; *school life* is the most vital part of education.

To such efforts the Indian girl responds almost incredibly. Whatever her faults—and she has many—she is never bored. Her own background is so narrow that school opens to her a new world of surprise. "Isn't it wonderful!" is the constant reaction to the commonplaces of science. No less wonderful to her is the liberty of thinking and acting for herself that self-government brings.

Seeta loves her home, but before a month is over its close confinement palls and she writes back, "I am living like a Muhammadan woman. I wish it were the last day of vacation." Her father is shocked by her desire to be up and doing. He calls on the school principal and complains, "I don't know what to make of my daughter. Why is she not like her mother? Are not cooking and sewing enough for any woman? Why has she these strange ideas about doing all sorts of things that her mother never wanted to do?" Then the principal tries to explain patiently that new wine cannot be kept in old bottles, and that unless the daughter were to he different from the mother it was hardly worth while to send her for secondary education. So, when the long holiday is over, Seeta returns with a fresh appreciation of what education means in her life; and we know that when *her* daughters come home for vacation, it will be to a mother with sympathy and understanding.

The girls' loyalty to their school is at times almost pathetic. An American teacher writes, "One moonlight night when I was walking about the grounds talking with some of the oldest girls, one of them caught my hand, and turned me about toward the school, which, even under the magic of the Indian moon, did not seem a particularly beautiful sight to me. 'Amma' (mother), she said, in a voice quivering with emotion, 'See how beautiful our school is! When I stand out here at night and look at it through the trees, it gives me such a feeling *here*,' and she pressed her hand over her heart.

"'Do you think it is only beautiful at night?' one of the other girls asked indignantly, and all joined in enthusiastic affirmations of its attractions even at high noon,—which all goes to show how relative the matter is. I, with my background of Wellesley lawns and architecture, find our school a hopelessly unsanitary makeshift to be endured patiently for a few years longer, but to these girls with their background of wretchedly poor village homes it is in its bare cleanliness, as well as in its associations, a veritable place of 'sweetness and light.'"

Athletics.

Organized play is one of the gifts that school life brings to India. It, too, has to be learned, for the Indian girl has had no home training in initiative. The family or the caste is the unit and she is a passive member of the group, whose supreme duty is implicit obedience. One Friday when school had just reopened after the Christmas vacation, one of the teachers came to the principal and said, "May we stop all classes this afternoon and let the children play? You see," as she saw remonstrance forthcoming, "it's just *because* it's been vacation. They say they have been so long at home and there has been no chance to play." Classes were stopped, and all the school played, from the greatest unto the least, until the newly aroused instinct was satisfied.

Basket ball had an interesting history in one school. At first the players were very weak sisters, indeed. The center who was knocked down wept as at a personal affront, and the defeated team also wept to prove their penitence for their defeat. But gradually the team learned to play fair, to take hard knocks, and to cheer the winners. They grew into such "good sports" that when one day an invading cow, aggrieved at being hit in the flank by a flying ball, turned and knocked the goal thrower flat on the ground, the interruption lasted only a few minutes. The prostrate goal-thrower recovered her breath, got over her fright, and, while admiring friends chased the cow to a safe distance, the game went on to the finish.

Dramatics.

The dramatic instinct is strong and the school girl actress shines, whether in the role of Ophelia or Ramayanti. In India among Hindus or Christians, in school or church or village, musical dramas are frequently composed and played and hold unwearied audiences far into the night. Among Christians there is a great fondness for dramatizing Bible narratives. Joseph, Daniel, and the Prodigal Son appear in wonderful Indian settings, "adapted" sometimes almost beyond recognition. They show interesting likeness to the miracle and mystery plays of the Middle Ages. There is the same naive presentation; the same introduction of the buffoon to offset tragedy with comedy; the same tendency to overemphasize the comic parts until all sense of reverence is lost. In some respects India and Mediaeval Europe are not so far apart.

A high school class one night presented part of the old Tamil drama of Harischandra. The heroine, an exiled queen, watches her child die before her in the forest. Having no money to pay for cremation on the burning ghat, she herself gathers firewood, builds a little pyre, and with such tears and lamentations as befit an Oriental woman lays her child's body on the funeral pile. Just as the fire is lighted and the corpse begins to burn, the keeper of the burning ghat appears and, with anger at this trespass, kicks over the pyre, puts the fire out, and throws the body aside. Just at this moment Chandramathy sees in him the exiled king, her husband and lord, and the father of her dead child. There are tearful recognitions; together they gather again the scattered firewood, rebuild the pyre, and share their common grief.

The play was given in a dimly lighted court, with simple costumes and the crudest stage properties. But one spectator will not soon forget the schoolgirl heroine whose masses of black hair swept to her knees. She lived again all the pathos, the anger and despair and reconciliation of the old tale, and her audience thrilled with her as at the touch of a tragedy queen.

Student Government.

Co-operation in school government and discipline is one of the most educational experiences that an Indian girl can pass through. To feel the responsibility for her own actions and those of her schoolmates, to form impersonal judgments that have no relation to one's likes and dislikes, these are lessons found not between the covers of text-books, but at the very heart of life-experience. Under such moral strain and stress character develops, not as a hothouse growth of unreal dreams and theories, but as the sturdy product of life situations.

Some schools divide themselves into groups, each of which elects a "queen" to represent and to rule. The queens with elected teachers and the principal form the governing body, before which all questions of discipline come for settlement. Great is the office of a queen. She is usually well beloved, but also at times well hated, for the "Court" occasionally dispenses punishments far heavier than the teachers alone would dare to inflict and its members often realize the truth of Shakespeare's statement, "Uneasy lies the head that wears a crown."

[Illustration: PRIESTS OF THE HINDU TEMPLE.]

The "Court" is now in session and has two culprits before its bar. Abundance has been found to have a cake of soap and a mirror, not her own, shut up in her box. Lotus copied her best friend's composition and handed it in as hers. What shall be done to the two? Discussion waxes hot. The play hour passes. Shouts and laughter come in from the tennis court and the basket ball field. Every one is having a good time save the culprits and the four queens, who pay the penalty of greatness and bear on their young shoulders the burdens of the world. Evidence is hard to collect, for the witnesses disagree among themselves. Then there are other complications. Abundance stole *things* which you can see and touch, while Lotus's theft was only one of intangible thoughts. Furthermore, Abundance comes from a no-account family, quite "down and out," while Lotus is a pastor's daughter and as such entitled to due respect and deference. And still further, nobody likes Abundance, while Lotus is very popular and counts one of the queens as her intimate friend. Much time passes, the supper bell rings, and the players troop noisily indoors, but the four burdened queens still struggle with their dawning sense of justice. At last, as the swift darkness drops, the case is closed and judgment pronounced. Much time has been consumed, but four girls have learned a few of life's big lessons, not found in books, such as: that thoughts are just as real as things; that likes and dislikes have nothing to do with matters of discipline; that a girl of a "way up" family should have more expected of her than one who is "down and out." Perhaps that experience will count more than any "original" in geometry.

Student Government also brings about a wonderful comradeship between teachers and pupils. Out of it has grown such a sense of friendly freedom as found expression in this letter written to its American teacher by a Junior Class who were more familiar with the meter of Evangeline than with the geometry lesson assigned.

Dear Miss———:

We are the Math. students who made you lose your temper this morning, and we feel very sorry for that. We found that we are the girls who must be blamed. We ought to have told you the matter beforehand, but we didn't, so please excuse us for the fault which we committed and we realize now. Our love to you.

V Form Math. Girls.

P.S. We would like to quote a poem which we are very much interested in telling you:

> "What is that that ye do, my children?
> What madness has seized you this morning?
> Seven days have I labored among you,
> Not in word alone, but showing the figures on the
>   board.
> Have you so soon forgotten all the definitions of *Loci*?
> Is this the fruit of my teaching and laboring?"

Co-operative Housekeeping.

Co-operation is needed not only in "being good," but also in eating and drinking and keeping clean. There are school families in India where every member from the "queen" to the most rollicking five-year-old has her share in making things go. The queen takes her turn in getting up at dawn to see that the "water set" is at the well on time; five-year-old Tara wields her diminutive broom in her own small corner, and each is proud of her share. There is in Indian life an unfortunate feud between the head and the hand. To be "educated" means to be lifted above the degradation of manual labor; to work with one's hands means something lacking in one's brain. Not seldom does a schoolboy go home to his village and sit idle while his father reaps the rice crop. Not seldom does an "educated" girl spend her vacation in letter writing and crochet work while her "uneducated" mother toils over the family cooking.

Girls, however, who have spent hours over the theories of food values, balanced meals, and the nutrition of children, and other hours over the practical working out of the theories in the big school family, go home with a changed attitude toward the work of the house. Siromony writes back at Christmas time, "The first thing I did after reaching home was to empty out the house and whitewash it."

Ruth's letter in the summer vacation ends, "We have given our mother a month's holiday. All she needs to do is to go to the bazaar and buy supplies. My sister and I will do all the rest."

On Christmas day, Miracle, who is spending her vacation at school, all on her own initiative gets up at three in the morning to kill chickens and start the curry for the orphans' dinner, so that the work may be well out of the way before time for the Christmas tree and church.

Golden Jewel begs the use of the sewing machine in the Mission bungalow. All the days before Christmas her bare feet on the treadle keep the wheels whirring. Morning and afternoon she is at it, for Jewel has a quiver full of little brothers and sisters, and in India no one can go to church on Christmas without a new and holiday-colored garment. One after another they come from Jewel's deft fingers and lie on the floor in a rainbow heap. When Christmas Eve comes all are finished—except her own. On Christmas morning all the family are in church at that early service dearest to the Indian Christian, with its decorations of palm and asparagus creeper, its carols and rejoicings and new and shining raiment. In the midst sits Jewel and her clothes to the most seem shabby, but to those who know she is the best dressed girl in the whole church, for she is wearing a new spiritual garment of unselfish service.

[Illustration: Tamil Girls Preparing for College]

[Illustration: The Village of the Seven Palms]

The Indian Girl's Religion.

To the Indian schoolgirl religion is the natural atmosphere of life. She discusses her faith with as little self-consciousness as if she were choosing the ingredients for the next day's curry. She knows nothing of those Western conventions that make it "good form" for us to hide all our emotions, all our depth of feeling, under the mask of not caring at all. She has none of that inverted hypocrisy which causes us to take infinite pains to assure our world that we are vastly worse than we are. What Lotus feels she expresses simply, naturally, be it her interest in biology, her friendship for you, or her response to the love of the All-Father. And that response is deep and genuine. There is a spiritual quality, an answering vibration, which one seldom finds outside the Orient. You lead morning prayers and to pray is easy, because in those schoolgirl worshippers you feel the mystic quality of the East leaping up in response. You teach a Bible class and the girls' eager

[Illustration: BASKETBALL AT ISABELLA THOBURN COLLEGE, LUCKNOW]

"Among you as He that serveth."

Religious emotion may find one of its normal outlets in personal right-living. That is good as far as it goes, but yet not enough. It must seek expression also in making life better for other people. The Indian schoolgirl lives in the midst of a vast social laboratory, surrounded by problems that are overwhelmingly intricate. What is her education worth? Nothing, if it leads to a cloistered seclusion; everything, if it brings her into vital healing touch with even one of its needs.

The spirit of Christian social service opens many doors. There are Sunday afternoons to be spent with the shy pupils of the High Caste Girls' Schools at the opposite end of town. In the outcaste village beside the rice fields we may find the other end of the social scale—twenty or thirty little barbarians whose opening exercises must start off with a compulsory bath at the well.

Vacation weeks at home are bristling with opportunity—the woman next door whose forgotten art of reading may be revived; the bride in the next street who longs to learn crochet work; the little troop of neighbor children who crowd the house to learn the haunting strains of a Christian lyric. A cholera epidemic breaks out, and, instead of blind fear of a demon-goddess to be placated, there is practical knowledge as to methods of guarding food and drinking water. The baby of the house is ill and, instead of exorcisms and branding with hot irons, there is a visit to the nearest hospital and enough knowledge of hygienic laws to follow out the doctor's directions.

Rebecca teaches a class of small boys in the outcaste Sunday school that gives preliminary baths. On this particular Sunday, however, she starts out armed not with the picture roll and lyric book, but with a motley collection of soap and clean rags, cotton swabs and iodine and ointment.

"Amma," says Rebecca, "in the little thatched house, the fourth beyond the school, I saw a boy whose head is covered with sores. May Zipporah teach my class to-day, while I go and treat the sores, as I have learned to do in school?" So Rebecca, following in the steps of Him who sent out His disciples not only to preach but also to heal, attacks one of the little strongholds of dirt and disease and carries it by storm. No young surgeon after his first successful major operation was ever prouder than Rebecca when the next Sunday evening she rushes into the bungalow, eyes shining, to report her cure complete.

Is there somewhere an American girl who longs to "do things"? A little plumbing—or its equivalent in a land where no plumbing is; a little bossing of the carpenter, the mason, the builder; a great deal of "high finance" in raising one dollar to the purchasing power of two; a deal of administration with need for endless tact; the teaching of subjects known and unknown,—largely the latter; a vast amount of mothering and a proportionate return in the love of children; days bristling with problems, and nights when one sinks into bed too tired to think or feel—there you have it, with much more. More because it means opportunity for creative work—creative as one helps to mould the new education of new India; creative as one reverently helps to fashion some of the lives that are to be new India itself. More too, as the rebound comes back to one's self in a life too full for loneliness, too obsessing for self-interest. Does it pay? Try it for yourself and see.

One bright noon in North India, sixty years ago, a young missionary on an evangelistic tour among the villages paused to rest by the wayside. As he paced up and down beneath the tamarind trees, pondering the problem of India's womanhood, shut in the zenanas beyond the reach of the Gospel which he was bringing to the little villages, there fell at his feet a feather from a vulture's wing. Picking it up, he whimsically cut it into a quill. Thinking that his sister in far-away America might like a letter from so strange a pen, he went into his tent and wrote to her. He told her of the millions of girls shut up in those "citadels of heathenism," the zenanas of India,—a problem which only Christian women might hope to solve. Half playfully, half in earnest, he added, "Why don't you come out and help?" As swift as wind and wave permitted was Isabella Thoburn's answer, "I am coming as soon as the way opens!"

Already a group of women, stirred to the depths by the words of Mrs. Edwin W. Parker and Mrs. William Butler, returned missionaries from India, were forming a Society to help the women and girls of Christless lands. At the first public meeting of this Woman's Foreign Missionary Society of the Methodist Episcopal Church, though but twenty women were present with but three hundred dollars in the treasury, when they learned that Isabella Thoburn,—gifted, consecrated, wise, was ready to go to India, they exclaimed, "Shall we lose Miss Thoburn because we have not the needed money in our hands to send her? No, rather let us walk the streets of Boston in our calico dresses, and save the expense of more costly apparel!" Thus was answered the letter written with the feather from the vulture's wing by the wayside in India. In 1870, Isabella Thoburn gathered six little waifs into her first school in India, a one-roomed building in the noisy, dusty bazaar of Lucknow. From this brave venture have grown the Middle School, the High School, and finally in 1886 the first woman's Christian College in all Asia, housed in the Ruby Garden, Lal Bagh. Here for thirty-one years Isabella Thoburn lived and loved and labored for the girls of India.

CHAPTER THREE

I. THE GARDEN OF HID TREASURE

Prelude: Why go to College?

"Why should an Indian girl want a college education?" queried Mary Smith, as she listened to her roommate's account of the "Lighting of the Christmas Candles." "I can see why she would need to learn to read and write, and even a high school course I wouldn't mind; but college seems to me perfectly silly, and an awful waste of good money. Why, from our own home high school there are only six of us at college."

Mary Smith, fresh from "Main Street," may be less provincial than she sounds. Her question puts up a real problem. When only one girl in one hundred has a chance at the Three R's, is it right to "waste money" on giving certain others the chance to delve into psychology and higher mathematics? When there is not bread enough to go around, why should some of the family have cake and pudding?

Something less than a hundred years ago, similar questions were vexing the American public. Those were the days when Mary Lyon fought her winning battle against the champions of the slogan "The home is woman's sphere," the days in which the pioneers of women's education foregathered from the rocky farmslopes of New England, and Mt. Holyoke came into being. Mary Smith, who is duly born, baptized, vaccinated, and registered for Vassar, the last requiring no more volition on her part than the first, realizes little of the ancient struggle that has made her privilege a matter of course.

They are much the same old arguments that must be gone over again to justify college education for our sisters of the East. Rather say argument, in the singular, for there is just one that holds, and that is the possibilities for service that such education opens up.

High schools there must be in India, but who will teach them? American and English women have never yet gone out to India in such numbers as to staff the schools they have founded, nor would there be funds to support them if they did. Travel through India to-day and you will find girls' schools staffed either with under-qualified women teachers, or else with men whose academic qualifications are satisfactory, but who, being men, cannot fill the place where a woman is obviously needed. What could be more contradictory than to find a Christian girls' school, supported largely by American money, but staffed by Hindu men, just because no Christian women with necessary qualifications are available?

Hospitals there must be, but where are the doctors to conduct them? Here again, foreign doctors can fill the need of the merest fraction of India's suffering womankind. But the American doctor can multiply herself in just one way. Give her a Medical College, well equipped and staffed, and a body of Indian girls with a sufficient background of general education, and instead of one doctor and one hospital you will find countless centres of healing springing up in city and small town and along the roadside where the doctor passes by.

Leadership there must be among the women of the New India. Where will it be found but among those women whose powers of initiative have been developed by the four years of life in a Christian college? Church workers, pastors' wives, social workers, child welfare promoters, where can you find them in India? Here and there, scattered in unlikely places, where educated women, married and home-making, yet let their surplus energy flow out into neighborhood betterment.

Mothers of families there must be, and far be it from me to say that non-college women fail in that high office. There comes before me one mother of fourteen children who has never seen the inside of a college classroom, yet whom it would be hard to excel in her qualities of motherliness. But, other things being equal, it is to the Christian, educated mothers that we turn to find the life of the ideal home, with real comradeship between wife and husband, with intelligent understanding of the children, and the coveting for them of the best that education can give.

One other question Mary Smith may rightly ask. What about the men's colleges already existing? Will co-education not work in India?

To a certain limited extent it has. Rukkubai, with her too brief years of freedom, proved its possibility. Others there have been, pioneer souls, who pushed their way into lecture halls crowded with men, took notes in the dark and undesirable remnants of space allotted to them, and by dint of perseverance and hard work passed the examinations of the University and carried off the coveted degree.

They were courageous women, deserving admiration. They won knowledge, sometimes at heavy cost of health and nerve power. They helped to make women's education possible. But what of the fairer side of college life could they ever know? They were accepted always on sufferance; they never "belonged." One such pioneer was a friend of mine. In many walks and talks she told me of life in a men's college under the patronage of the Maharajah of a native state. Loyal to her college, and proud of the treasures of opportunity it had opened to her, she yet sighed for what she had missed. "When I see the life of the girls in the Women's

Christian College at Madras," she said, "I feel that I have never been to college."

Three times the girls and women of America have reached out hands across the sea and either founded or helped to found Christian schools of higher education for the women of India, with the belief that they have a right to the knowledge of the spiritual truth which has brought to Christian women of America development in righteousness, freedom of faith, a personal knowledge of God through Jesus Christ, and the blessed hope of immortality.

Isabella Thoburn College, Lucknow, 1886.

The Women's Christian College, Madras, 1915.

The Vellore Medical School, 1918.

These three names and dates are red-lettered in the history of international friendship, for through them the college women of America and India are joined into one fellowship of knowledge and service.

[Illustration: BIOLOGY CLASS AT LUCKNOW COLLEGE
Head of Class Leaning on Table, and Nine Students Dissecting Nine Rabbits]

LUCKNOW

Lal Bagh.

A dusty journey of a night and almost a day brings you from Calcutta across the limitless Ganges plains to Lucknow, capital of the ancient kingdom of Oudh. Every tourist visits it, making a pious pilgrimage first to the Residency, where in the midst of green lawns and banyan trees the scarred ruins tell of the unforgettable Mutiny days of '57; and then to the nearby cemetery, where the dead sleep among the jasmines. Then, if his hours are wisely chosen, the traveler drives back to the town at sunset when palace towers and cupolas, mosque minarets and domes are silhouetted against the blazing west in an unrivalled skyline.

The tourist returns to the bazaars and in the midst of them, amid the dust and clatter of *ekkas* and *tongas*, probably passes by a sight more interesting than Residency ruins and abandoned palaces—inasmuch as it deals with the living present rather than the dead past. It was in Lal Bagh, the Ruby Garden of hid treasure, that the Nawab Iq bal-ud-dowler, Lord Chamberlain to the first king of Oudh, hid, according to report, great caskets of silver rupees, with a huge ruby possessed of magic virtues, and left behind him a sheet of detailed directions for finding the treasure, with, alas, a postscript to explain that all the careful directions were quite wrong, being intended to mislead the would-be discoverer. It was again in Lal Bagh that Isabella Thoburn founded her school for Indian girls, and in 1886 opened the classes of the first women's college for India to possess residence accommodation and a staff of women teachers. The buried rupees and the magic ruby have never been unearthed; instead these years of Lal Bagh history have witnessed the discovery of richer treasure in the minds and hearts of young women, set free from age-long repressions and sent out to share their riches with a world in need.

You enter Lal Bagh's gates and find yourself before a stretch of dull red buildings whose wide-arched verandahs are built to keep out the fierce suns of May In November the sun has lost its terrors, and you rejoice in its warmth as it shines upon the gardens with their riot of color—yellow and white chrysanthemums, roses, and masses of flaming poinsettias, surely a fair setting for the girls who walk amid its changing loveliness.

Cosmopolitan Atmosphere.

As you leave the setting and for a few days merge yourself into the life that is going on within, there are a few outstanding impressions that fasten upon you and persistently mingle with Lal Bagh memories. Of these, perhaps, the foremost is the cosmopolitan atmosphere. Here you have on the one hand a group of American college women representing no one locality, no narrow section of American life, but drawn from east and west, north and south. On the other side, you see a body of nearly sixty Indian students whose homes range all the way from Ceylon to the Northwest frontier, from Singapore to Bombay.

What of the result? It is an atmosphere where East and West meet, not in conflict, but in a spirit of give and take, where each re-inforces the other. It is probably due to this friendly clash of ideas that the "typical" student at Isabella Thoburn strikes the observer as of no "type" at all, but a person whose ideas are her own and who has a gift for original thinking rare in one's experience of Indian girls. In the class forums that were held during my visit the most striking element was the difference of opinion, and its free expression.

Scholarship. Lal Bagh is no longer satisfied with the production of mere graduates. Her ambition is now reaching out to post-graduate study, made possible by the gift of an American fellowship. The first to receive this honor are two Indian members of the faculty, one of them Miss Thillayampalam, Professor of Biology, whose home is in far-off Ceylon at the other end of India's world. Henceforth, America may expect to find each year one member of the Lal Bagh family enrolled in some school of graduate work. Such work, however, is not to be confined to a scholarship in a foreign land, for this year the college enrolls Regina Thumboo, its first candidate for the degree of M.A. Her parents, originally from the South, emigrated from Madras to Singapore. There Regina was born, the youngest of five children. The father, a civil engineer in the employ of a local rajah was ambitious for his children, and, seeing in Regina a child of unusual promise, sent her first to a Singapore school, then on the long journey across to Calcutta and inland to Lucknow. At Lal Bagh she stands foremost in scholarship. When she has completed her M.A. in history and had her year of advanced work in some American university, she plans to return to the faculty of her *Alma Mater*.

Social Questions.

Scholarship at Isabella Thoburn College does not deal exclusively with the dusty records of dead languages and bygone civilizations. It is linked up with present questions, and is alive to the changing India of to-day. Among the matters discussed during my visit were such as: the substitution of a vernacular for English in the university course; the possibility of a national language for all India; the advisability of co-education; and the place of the unmarried woman in New India. To report all that the girls said and wrote would require a book for itself, but so far as space allows we will let the girls speak for themselves.

Co-education.

The Senior Class of eight discussed co-education with great interest, and when the vote was taken five were in the affirmative and only three in the negative.

[Illustration]

The following paper voices the objections to co-education as expressed by one especially thoughtful student:

"Co-education is an excellent thing, but it can only work successfully in those highly civilized countries where intellectual and moral strength and freedom of intercourse control the lives and thoughts of the student bodies. Unfortunately these fundamental principles of co-education are sadly lacking in India.

"Although woman's education is being pushed forward with considerable force, for many years to come the girls will still be a small minority in comparison with the number of boys. Besides, in two or three cases where Indian girls have had the privilege of studying with the boys, they have told me that, in spite of immensely enjoying the competitive spirit and broadminded behavior of the boys, they always felt a certain strain and strangeness in their company. One student attended a history class for full two years and yet she never got acquainted with one single boy in her class. There is no social intercourse between the two parties. If each side does not stand on its own dignity in constant fear of overstepping the bounds of etiquette and courtesy, their reputation is bound to be marred."

The arguments for the other side are presented as well. The American reader may be interested to see that the Indian college girl does not consider Western ways perfect, but is quite ready to criticize the manners and morals of her American cousin.

"Co-education cannot burst upon India like lightning. It has to grow gradually in society; and until there is a perfect understanding and sympathy between the sexes, this system will not work.

"Again, co-education should not begin from college. The girls come in from high schools where they are locked up and have no contact with the outside world; and if they come into such colleges when many of them are immature, there will be not only a complete failure of the system, but the result will be fatal in many cases. So the system should be introduced from the primary department and worked up through the high schools and colleges.

"First, there is the question of chivalry, which is a problem that Indian men should solve for themselves. But how are they to solve it? If they study with women, chivalry would become natural to them.

"On the other hand, a woman has to learn how to receive a man's attention—how far to go in her behavior. The question now is, where can she learn this? Isn't it by mixing and mingling in a place where she feels that she is not inferior to man? It is in an educational institution that this equality is most keenly felt.

"Closely allied with chivalry is the question of modesty. It is commonly said that Indian women have a poise, quietness, and reserve different to that in Western women.

"Boldness in women is another fact connected with the above. Indian men and women should not try to follow Western manners. They have hereditary manners which should not be deserted. Indian women can keep their modesty and reserve even while mixing with men. If co-education is made a slow development this difficulty will not appear.

"Secondly, this system will give more facilities to woman for various kinds of occupation. She will then realize that her education is not confined to her home merely, but that she has a right to contribute to humanity just as big a share as any man. With this realization there will come efforts on her part to better the condition of her country by doing her little share. How much a woman can do who has a firm conviction that she is not inferior to any one in this life, but that she is a contributor to her country, whichsoever vocation she follows in life, in that she can do her share!

"The third point is that early marriage and widowhood will be lessened in a large degree. While education will teach men and women to reverence their parents and always consult them, at the same time they will learn to choose for themselves. By coming in contact with the opposite sex, they will learn to decide their marriage themselves; and choosing does not come at an early and immature age. Thus child widowhood, too, will be decreased. Then, too, the widows will be able to work for their livelihood if they don't wish to marry again."

Purdah.

To the North India girl, perhaps the most vexing social question is that of *purdah*. How can education reach women who live shut away from the sky and the sun and the lives of men? On the other hand, if after the seclusion of a thousand years freedom were suddenly thrust upon women not even trained to desire it, who can measure the disaster that would follow? Where can the vicious circle be broken, and how?

Tiny arcs of its circumference have been broken already. Lal Bagh includes in its family not only its majority of Christian girls, but also a scattering of Hindus and Muhammadans who have made more or less of a break with ancestral customs.

One among these is a member of the Sophomore Class, Omiabala Chatterji of Allahabad. Of Brahman parentage, she was fortunate in having a father of liberal views, who was ambitious for his daughter's education.

He died when Omiabala was but three years old, but not before he had passed on to his wife his hopes for the future of the little daughter. The mother, with no experience of school life herself, but only the limited opportunity of a little teaching in her own home, yet entered into the father's ambitions. From childhood Omiabala was taught that hers was not to be the ordinary life of the Brahman woman—she was set apart by her father's wish, dedicated to the service of her people. So the years came and went, and instead of wedding festivities the child was sent away on the journey to Lucknow, to enter into a strange, new life. There followed weeks of homesickness and longing, then gradual adjustment, then glad acceptance of new opportunity. Omiabala now talks enthusiastically of her future plans for work among her own people—plans for the education of Brahman girls, and for marriage reform such as shall make this possible.

[Illustration: VILLAGE PEOPLE.]

The Freshman Class had a spirited discussion as to the benefits and evils of the purdah system. Opinions ranged all the way from that of the zealous young reformer who wished it abolished at once and for all; through advocates of slow changes lasting ten, twenty or even thirty years; all the way to the young Hindu wife, who would never see it done away with, "because women would become disobedient to their husbands."

Here are some of the pros and cons. A Hindu student writes:

"I maintain that the purdah system should not be done away with altogether, for it will upset the whole foundation of the Hindu principle of 'dharm' or how a woman should act and behave before she is called a good and honorable woman. Sometimes, when a woman is given much freedom and liberty and is allowed to go wherever she pleases, she begins to take advantage of such opportunities and does those things which might bring disgrace to the family. The question of education should not be brought up in connection with the purdah, for even the educated ladies are apt to fall in the same temptation as the uneducated ones when the purdah system is removed altogether. The purdah system has done much to maintain the honor and respect of the higher class ladies. The low class women who are always abroad working among men and in the midst of throngs of people are not educated at all and have as much freedom as their men have. So we can conclude that the purdah system only exists among higher classes of people and those who care much for the honor and respect of their family. The higher a family is the more it will be particular about this system."

The following paragraph expresses the views of a Muhammadan Freshman:

"Among us, that is the Muslims, purdah is very strict. Ladies need purdah at present, for the men are not civilized enough. Besides, the purdah system should be gradually abolished. If too much freedom is given all at once, ladies won't know how to behave and they will be an hindrance in further progress. Education is at the back of progress. Girls should first be educated and given liberty gradually. Though we Muslim girls have come to Christian colleges and don't observe purdah, yet we are very careful of how we should make the best of it and show a good example by our personality and behavior so that the people who criticize us may not have anything to say. I think if all of us try hard to abolish this system it will take us at least twenty years to do it. No matter what happens I don't approve of ladies mixing *very* much with gentlemen.

"There are certainly many disadvantages in the purdah system. For instance, it makes ladies quite helpless and dependent. They cannot go out to get any thing or travel even if they are in great necessity. They do not know the streets and roads, so they cannot run away to save their honor or life. Men seem to become their right hand and feet. They do not know, often, what is going on outside their homes and do not enjoy the beauty of nature, and live an uneventful life. This seems to make the ladies lazy and they always keep planning marriages. This is the chief reason of the early marriage of girls among the Muslims. The girl herself has nothing to do, so they think it best for her to get married."

With these it is interesting to compare the views of a Christian student, a young pastor's wife, who along with the care of home and children is now receiving the higher education of which she was deprived in her schoolgirl days.

"The genius of the East will take some time to be taught the social customs of the West. To an Indian it would be a horrible idea if his sister or daughter or wife will go out to tea or supper or dance with a young man who is neither related nor a close friend of the family. India will fondly preserve its genius.

"Indian leaders look with alarm at the possibility of a female India of the type of the West. They would like the purdah system to be removed, females to be educated, to get the franchise, and still for them to keep their modesty. There are many who would like to break this barrier, but it would be disastrous for India to arrive at such a state within fifteen or twenty years when ninety-nine out of one hundred women are illiterate. Education is essential and as long as Indian women, the future mothers of India, do not realize their responsibility, it is much better and wiser that they should remain behind the scene.

"The help we can give in bringing about this great reform is to show by our example. Freedom does not mean simply coming out of purdah and taking undue advantage and misuse of liberty. We who have done away with our purdah should not be stumbling blocks to others. Freedom guided and governed by the Spirit of God is the only freedom and every true citizen ought to help to bring it about."

Social Service.

Lal Bagh students are interested not only in the theories of social reform; they are taking a direct part in the application of these theories through the means of social service, not put off for some future "career," but carried on during the busy weeks of college life. Nor is such service merely social; through it all the Christian motive holds sway. We will let one of the students tell in her own words what they are attempting.

"'Cleanliness is next to godliness' is the first lesson we teach in our social and Christian service fields. Both in our work in the city and in our own servants' compound, we emphasize personal cleanliness and that of the home, and have regular inspection of servants' homes.

"Religious instruction is given to non-Christian children and women in various sections of the city in separate classes. Side by side with these, they are given tips about doctoring simple ailments, and taught how to take precautions at the time of epidemics like cholera, typhoid, etc. Lotions, fever mixtures, cough mixtures, quinine, etc., are given to the poorer depressed classes, as also clothes and soap to the needy ones.

"In the servants' compound plots have been provided for gardening, and provision made for the children's play, and pictures given to parents as prizes for tidy homes. Soap and clothes and medicines are given here also; a special series of lectures on diseases and the evils of drink has been started. A lecture a week is given—cholera, malaria, typhoid fever, dysentery have been touched on—lantern slides and charts and pictures have been used for illustration. On Saturday nights the Christian servants have song-service and prayer meeting, and on Sunday noon a Bible class. Each of these is conducted by a teacher assisted by girls of the College.

"There is opportunity for service for people of all tastes—those who prefer teaching how to read and write, for sewing, for care of the health, care of the baby, avoiding sickness, nursing the sick ... but in every case devotion, enthusiasm, and a sympathetic Christian spirit are needed. Our motive both among our own Christian servants and those who reside in the city and are non-Christians is to serve the least of our needy fellowmen according to the wishes of our Master, and to enlighten and uplift our less fortunate neighbors through the avenues of Christian social service."

An interesting practical suggestion is the following:

"In our Social Service class, which is held every Thursday, there has come up a suggestion about opening up a few Purdah Parks for Indian ladies. It is very essential that Indian women should have some places, where they can take recreation and have some social intercourse with one another, also that the rich and poor may all meet and be brought into sympathy with one another.

"There is a Park right in front of our College, and we have suggested that, if this particular Park is made into a Purdah Park once a week, then we college girls interested in social service work can form a committee and look after the different arrangements, such as the water supply, games, playthings for children, etc.

"We have drawn up a petition and this will be signed by the influential ladies of this place, such as the wives of the Professors of our Lucknow University, and then it will be presented to the Lucknow Improvement Trust Committee.

"We all hope that this petition will be granted, and our sisters will have more of social life and hygienic advantages, to help make stronger mothers and stronger children."

Nor do the girls of Isabella Thoburn College forget all these interests when vacation days come round. This tells something of holiday opportunity. How do our summer vacations compare with it? "How apt one is to slacken and get a little selfish in planning out a programme for a holiday. One is not tied down to the usual duties and routine of school work, and plans are made as to the best possible way of spending the days for one's own pleasure and relaxation. The many little things that one's heart longs for, and for which there is no time during the busy days, are now looked forward to; a particular piece of needlework, a favorite book, some excursions to places of interest; all these and other things are likely to crowd out thoughts of our duties to others in making life a little better and some one a little happier each day.

"And yet a holiday is the time when one can more freely give oneself to others, for opportunities of helpful service offer themselves in the very holiday pursuits, if one has eyes for them.

"Rooming in a home where many mothers have still many more children, one would feel at first like escaping from the noise and commotion caused by crying babies, and yet here are some opportunities of service. It is never a wise plan to leave children to the entire care of ayahs. A very profitable hour may be spent in directing games when the little people build with their bricks gates and bridges, houses and castles, and the older ones listen with interest to some story of adventure. An hour spent in the open air under shady trees in this way would draw many a grateful heart, for there would be less crying, fewer quarrels, and a little more peace for all around.

"In these days when strikes are so common, many opportunities for social service offer themselves. It may be a postal strike. Now, not many of us like to be kept waiting for our mail, and, if the postmen are not bringing us our letters, we very soon contrive some means of getting them. I grant it isn't a very enviable job to be standing outside a delivery window awaiting the sorting of letters by a crew of girl guides and boy scouts, who are not any too serious about their work. But once the letters are secured and delivered at the neighboring homes of friends and others, it is something done, besides the satisfaction of being able to sit down and read your own letters as well as having the grateful appreciation from others.

"Again, a picnic has been planned to some far away hill. The party arrives; tiffin baskets are placed in some shady spot. One of the party wanders away to a little village not far off. She is soon surrounded by a group of scrubby children, who watch her with eyes full of curiosity and wonder. She dips her hand into the bag she has been carrying and brings out a handful of nuts and oranges, and, before sharing them with the children, she invites them to wash their scrubby, little hands and faces in the sparkling stream of clear, crystal water that is flowing through the valley. She gets to talking to them, and asks about their homes, and one little child leads her to a meagre, little, grassy hut in which her sick sister is lying. She hasn't any medicine with her, but she opens wide the door of the hut and lets the bright sunlight in. She strokes the little one's feverish brow, and sets to, and fixes up the bed and soon gets the sickroom, such as it is, clean and tidy. The mother is touched by the gentle kindliness of the stranger and confides her sorrows to her. Other homes are visited. People expecting the kind visitor brush up and tidy their huts.

"So the picnic excursion ends leaving a cleaner and happier spot nestling in among those mountainsides. Several visits are paid to the little village. The stranger is no longer a stranger, for she is now known and loved and is greeted by clean, happy, smiling children, and blessed by grateful mothers. And so in the home and in the office and in God's out-of-doors we can find opportunities for helping others."

[Illustration: GIRLS OF ALL CASTES MEET ON COMMON GROUND IN THE
CHRISTIAN COLLEGE.]

Eminent among the student body for maturity of thought and depth of Christian purpose is Shelomith Vincent. Many of these characteristics may be accounted for by her splendid inheritance. Her father was of the military caste, the son of a Zemindar, or petty rajah. At the time of the Mutiny he, a boy of ten years, ran away in the crowd and followed the mutineers on their long march from Lucknow to Agra, where he was rescued by a missionary and brought up in his family. Later, longing to know his past, the young man returned to Lucknow, found his relatives, weighed in the balance the claims of Hinduism and Christianity, and of his own accord decided for the latter. Later we see him a Sanskrit student in Benares, where he married his wife, a fifteen-year-old Brahman convert.

The Christian couple moved soon to the Central Provinces, where Mr. Vincent entered upon his twenty-five years of service as a Christian pastor, using his Sanskrit learning to interpret the message of Christianity to his Hindu friends. Yet it was in lowlier ways that his life was most telling. Settling in a peasant colony of a thousand so-called converts, only half-Christianized, the story of his labors and triumphs reads like that of Columba, or Boniface in early Europe. Through perils of robbers and perils of famine he labored on, building villages, digging wells, distributing American corn in famine days, reproving, teaching, guiding. All this I am telling, because it explains much of the daughter's quiet strength. One of ten children, she has spent many years in earning money to educate the younger brothers and sisters, and she is finishing her college course as a mature woman. Miss Vincent hopes that the American fellowship may one day be hers; and already her plans are developing as to the ways she will contrive to pass on her opportunities to her fellow countrywomen. Her heart is with those illiterate village women among whom her childhood was passed; her longing is to share with them the truth, the beauty, and the goodness with which Lal Bagh has filled her days.

Has Lal Bagh been a paying investment? One wishes that every one whose dollars have found expression in its walls might come to feel the indefinable spirit that pervades them, filling cold brick and mortar with life energy. For centuries philosophers searched for that Philosopher's Stone that was to transmute base metals into gold. In the world to-day there are those who have found a subtler magic that transforms dead gold and silver into warm human purposes and the Christ-spirit of service. That is the miracle one sees in daily process at Lal Bagh.

IN THE SECRET OF HIS PRESENCE

ELLEN LAKSHMI GOREH (*Lucknow College*)

In the secret of His presence how my soul delights to hide!
Oh, how precious are the lessons which I learn at Jesus' side!
Earthly cares can never vex me, neither trials lay me low;
For when Satan comes to tempt me, to the secret place I go.

When my soul is faint and thirsty, 'neath the shadow of His wing
There is cool and pleasant shelter, and a fresh and crystal spring;

And my Saviour rests beside me, as we hold communion
  sweet:
If I tried, I could not utter what He says when thus we meet.

  Only this I know: I tell Him all my doubts, my griefs and
  fears;
Oh, how patiently He listens! and my drooping soul He
  cheers:
Do you think He ne'er reproves me? What a false friend He
  would be,
If He never, never told me of the sins which He must see.

  Would you like to know the sweetness of the secret of the
  Lord?
Go and hide beneath His shadow: this shall then be your
  reward;
And whene'er you leave the silence of that happy meeting
  place,
You must mind and bear the image of the Master in your face.

[Illustration: SHELOMITH VINCENT]

LAL BAGH ALUMNAE RECORDS SHOW THE FOLLOWING:

The first Kindergarten in India.

The first college in India with full staff of women and residence accommodation.

The first Arya Samaj B.A. graduate.

The F.Sc. graduate who became the second woman with the B.Sc. degree in India.

The F.Sc. graduate who later graduated at the foremost Medical College in North India as the first Muhammadan woman doctor in India and probably in the world.

The first woman B.A. and the first Normal School graduate from Rajputana.

The first woman to receive her M.A. in North India.

The first Muhammadan woman to take her F.A. examination from the Central Provinces.

Probably the first F.A. student to take her examination in purdah.

The first Teachers Conference (held annually) in India.

The first woman's college to offer the F.Sc. course.

The first college to have on its staff an Indian lady.

The first woman (Lilavati Singh) from the Orient to serve on a world's Committee.

The first woman dentist.

The first woman agriculturist.

The first woman in India to be in charge of a Boys' High School.

A Lal Bagh graduate organized the Home Missionary Society which has developed into an agency of great service to the neglected Anglo-Indian community scattered throughout India.

The Lal Bagh student who took an agricultural course in America and is now helping convert wastes of the Himalaya regions into fruitful valleys.

Miss Phoebe Rowe, an Anglo-Indian who was associated with Lal Bagh in Miss Thoburn's time, was a wonderful influence in the villages of North India and carried the Christian message by her beautiful voice as well as her consecrated personality. She traveled in America, endearing India to many friends here. She is one—perhaps the most remarkable, however—of many Lal Bagh daughters who are serving as evangelists in faraway places.

FROM A STUDENT AT MADRAS WOMEN'S COLLEGE

"Your letter was handed to me as I returned from my evening hour of prayer, prayer for our school, special prayer for the problem God has called us to tackle together. I believe that the solution for many of our problems at school is to put things on a Christian foundation. We want workers who are real Christians and who love the Master as sincerely as they do themselves and serve Him for their love of Him. This may not be easy work for us to do, but if God is transforming the whole globe and moulding it from the 'new spiritual center,' namely,—Jesus Christ, it is certainly not hard for Him to accomplish it in this place. How He is going to do it I am blind to see. Let us put our feet on the one step that we see with the faith expressed in 'One step enough for me,' and the next step will flash before our eyes. One question that used to trouble me is, how we are to do the work. The poem by Edward Sill in 'The Manhood of the Master' cheers me up now as then with the thought that a broken sword flung away by a craven as useless was used by a king's son to win victory in the same battle. God will use it and perform His work. We have dedicated ourselves for His duty which is gripping our souls. He will use them according to His purpose."

CHAPTER FOUR

AN INTERNATIONAL ALLIANCE

Education and World Peace.

While statesmen discuss disarmament and politicians and newspaper editors foment race consciousness and mutual distrust, certain forces that never figure in newspaper headlines, that come "not with observation," are working with silent constructive power to bind nations together in ties of peace and good will. Among these silent forces are certain educational institutions. Columbia University has its Cosmopolitan Club, at whose Sunday night suppers you may meet representatives of forty to fifty nations, Occidental and Oriental. In the Near East, amid the race hatred and strife that set every man's hand against his fellow, the American Colleges at Constantinople and Beirut have stood foremost among the forces that produce unification and brotherhood.

During the war-scarred days of 1915, while nation was rising up against nation, there was founded in the city of Madras one of these international ventures in co-operation. Known to the world of India as the Women's Christian College of Madras, it might just as truthfully be called a Triangular Alliance in Education, for in it Great Britain including Canada, the United States, and India are joined together in educational endeavor. America may well admire what Britain has been doing during long years for India's educational advancement. Among England's more recent contributions to education in India none has been greater that the coming of Miss Eleanor McDougall from London University to take the principalship of this international college for women. Under her wise leadership British and American women have worked in one harmonious unit, and international co-operation has been transformed from theory to fact.

Where Missions Co-operate.

The Women's Christian College is not only international, it is also intermissionary. Supported by fourteen different Mission Boards, including almost every shade of Protestant belief and every form of church government, it stands not only for international friendship, but also as an outstanding evidence of Christian unity.

The staff and the student body are as varied as the supporting constituency. In the former, along with British and American professors are now two Indian women lecturers, Miss George, a Syrian Christian, who teaches history, and Miss Janaki, a Hindu, who teaches botany. Both are resident and a happy factor in the home life of the college. Among the students nine Indian languages are represented, ranging all the way from Burma to Ceylon, from Bengal to the Malabar Coast. From the last named locality come Syrian Christians in great numbers. This interesting sect loves to trace its history back to the days of the Apostle Thomas. Be that historical fact or merely a pious tradition, this sect can undoubtedly boast an indigenous form of Christianity that dates back to the early centuries of the Christian era; and it stands to-day in a place of honor in the Indian Christian community.

[Illustration: A road near the College]

[Illustration: The Potters' Shop
STREET SCENES IN MADRAS]

The Sunflower and the Lamp.

Perhaps much of the success which the College at Madras has achieved on the side of unity is due to the fact that her members are too busy to think or talk about it because their time is all filled up with actually doing things together. Expressing this spirit of active co-operation is the college motto, "Lighted to lighten"; the emblem in the shield is a tiny lamp such as may burn in the poorest homes in India. Below the lamp is a sunflower, whose meaning has been discussed in the college magazine by a new student. She says, "To-day the sunflower stands for very much in my mind. It is symbolic of this our College, for, as our amateur botanists tell us, the sunflower is not a flower, but a congregation of them. The tiny buds in the centre are our budding intellects. To-day they are in the making; to-morrow they will bloom like their sisters who surround them. Nourished from the same source, their fruit will be even likewise.

"Around these are the golden rays—each a tongue of fire to protect and inspire. There is none high or low amongst them, being all alike, and these are our tutors, and the sunflower itself turns to the sun, the great giver of life, for its inspiration, ever turning to him, never losing sight of his face. A force inexplicable draws the flower to the King of Day, even as our hearts are turned to Him at morn and at eve, be we East or West."

In a Garden.

It is fitting that the sunflower should bloom in a garden, and so it does. This time it is not a walled garden like that of Lal Bagh; the Women's

College is situated out from the city in a green and spacious suburb, where the little River Cooum wanders by its open spaces. The ten acres have much the air of an American college campus,—the same sense of academic quiet, of detachment from the work-a-day world. The whole compound is dominated by the tall, white columns of the old main building, which confer an air of distinction upon the whole place, as well they may, for have they not guarded successively government officials and Indian rajahs?

Nearby is the new residence hall, as modern as the other is historic. Three stories in height, its verandahs are in the form of a hollow square, and look out upon a courtyard gay with the bright-hued foliage of crotons and other tropical plants. Beyond is the garden itself, filled not with the roses and chrysanthemums of winter Lucknow, but with the perpetual summer foliage of spreading rain trees, palms, and long fronded ferns, with fluffy maidenhair between. In their season the purple masses of Bougainvillea, and the crimson of the Flamboya tree set the garden afire. In the evening when the girls are sitting under the trees or walking down the long vistas with the level sunbeams bringing out the bright colors of their draped *saris*, it brings to mind nothing so much as a scene from "The Princess" where among fair English gardens

"One walked reciting by herself, and one
In this hand held a volume as to read."

Student Organizations.

Yet life in the Women's College is not a cloistered retreat such as "The Princess" tried to establish, nor are its activities confined to the study of classics in a garden. Student organizations flourish here with a variety almost as great as in the West. There is, first of all, the College Committee, which corresponds roughly to our Scheme of Student Government. Its members are chosen from the classes and in their turn elect a President known as "Senior Student." She is the official representative of the whole student body. Communications from faculty to students pass through her, and she represents the College on state occasions, such as visits from the Viceroy or other Government officials. Various student committees are also elected to plan meetings for the Literary and Debating Societies, to organize excursions for "Seeing Madras," and to plan for athletic teams and contests. How well the last named have succeeded is proved by the silver cup carried off as a trophy by the College badminton team, which distinguished itself as the winner in last year's intercollegiate sports.

An unusual organization is the Star Club, which has been carried on for several years, with programme meetings once a month and bi-weekly groups for observation. No wonder that astrology and the beginnings of astronomy came from the Orient, or that Wise Men from the East found a Star as the sign to lead their journeying. Night after night the constellations rise undimmed in the clear sky and fairly urge the beholder to close acquaintance. A knowledge of them fills the sky with friendly forms and gives the student a new and lasting "hobby" that may be pursued anywhere, and kept through life. The Star Club has popularized its celestial interests by presenting to the College a pageant in three scenes, a "Dream of the Sun and Planets," in which the Earth Dweller is transported to the regions of the sky and holds long and intimate conversations with the various heavenly bodies. As the final scene, the planets slant in their relative positions, and the Signs of the Zodiac with shields take their places on each side of Father Sun.

The Natural history Club has interests ranging all the way from the theory of evolution to the names and songs of the common birds of Madras.

The Art Club not only does out-door sketching, but has entered upon a wide field in the study of Indian art and architecture. India is reviving a partly forgotten interest in her ancient arts and crafts and has much to offer the student, from the wonderful lines of the Taj Mahal to the Ahmadabad stone windows with their lace-like traceries; from the portraits of Moghal Emperors to the fine detail of South India temple carvings. Study in the Art Club means a new appreciation of the beauty found among one's own people.

The Dramatic and Musical Societies unite now and then in public entertainments, such as "Comus" which was given in honor of the women graduates of the whole Presidency at the time of the University Convocation. The Society repertoire of plays given during the last five years includes a considerable variety—dramatists so far apart as Shakespeare and Tagore; the old English moralities of "Everyman" and "Eager Heart"; the old Indian epic-dramas of "Sakuntala" and "Savitri"; together with Sheridan's "Rivals" and scenes from "Emma" and "Ivanhoe." The Musical Club specializes on Christmas carols, with which the College is wakened at four o'clock "on Christmas day in the morning."

The History Club sounds like an organization of research workers; on the contrary, its interests are bound up with the march of current events in India and the world. At the time when India was stirred by the visit of the Duke of Connaught and the launching of the Reform Government, this Club took to itself the rights of suffrage, elected its members to the first Madras Legislative Council, and after the elections were duly confirmed sat in solemn assembly to settle the affairs of the Province. They have also carried out equally dramatic representations of the English House of Lords and even the League of Nations.

"Lighted to Lighten."

The Young Women's Christian Association of the College among its many activities includes Bible classes in the vernacular which bring together students from the same language areas and after a week of purely English study and English chapel service serve as a link with home life and home conditions. Not only with home on the one side; on the other the Association ties them up with wider interests, with conferences that bring together students from all India, with activities that range all the way from teaching servants' children to read and translating Christian books into their own vernaculars to sending gifts of money to a suffering student in Vienna.

Social service is carried on along lines not very different from those pursued in Lucknow. Sunday schools, visits to outcaste villages, and lectures on health and cleanliness have their place. A new feature is the dispensing of simple medical help, which not only relieves the recipients, but teaches the students what they can do later when in their own homes. Another distinctive venture is the "Little School" in the college grounds, where volunteer workers take turns morning and evening in teaching the neighborhood children, and thus get their first taste of the joys and difficulties of the teacher's profession.

An interested girl thus expresses her ideas on the subject of social service. Her emphasis upon the positive side of life speaks well for her future accomplishment:

"Though the condition of the people is deplorable we need not despair of making matters better for them. Instead of giving the mere negative instructions that they should not drink, or be extravagant with their money, or get into the clutches of money lenders, we can do something positive. Some interesting diversions could be invented that would prevent men from frequenting drinking houses. With regard to their extravagance on certain occasions, we might suggest to them ways in which they could lessen items of expenditure. To prevent their being at the mercy of money lenders, co-operative societies may be started in order to lend money at a lower rate of interest; or to supply them with capital or with tools in order to start their work.

"To remove the other evil of ignorance with regard to health, we may go into the villages and give them practical lessons on cleanliness. We could tell them of the value of fresh air and give them other needful instructions.

"In doing social work of this kind, there are many principles we ought to have in mind. Instead of telling a poor man with no means of living that he should not steal it would be better to see that he is somehow placed beyond the reach of want. Another is that instead of merely imparting morality in negative form, it would be better to point out to them some positive way in which they could improve. More important than any of these principles is that instead of thinking of 'bestowing good' on the people, it would be more effective, if we co-operate with them and enlist their initiative, thus enabling them by degrees to be fit to manage their own affairs."

Applied Sociology.

Certain parts of the curriculum also tie up closely with community life. Economics and essay writing lead into fields of research. Essays and contributions to the College magazine, "The Sunflower," bear such titles as the "Social Needs of Kottayam District," which goes into the causes of poverty and distress in the writer's own locality, or "The Religion of the People of Kandy," written by a convert from Buddhism who knows from her own childhood experience the beauties and defects of that great religious system.

An intercollegiate essay prize was won by a Christian college girl who wrote on her own home town, "The Superstitions and Customs of the Village of Namakal." She writes:

"A set of villages would also be seen where the people are very much like the insects under a buried stone, which run underground, unable to see the light or to adapt themselves to the light. The moment the stone is turned up, so much accustomed are they to live in the darkness of superstition and unbelief that they think they would be better off to go on so, and refuse to accept the light rays of science, education, and civilization, which are willingly given them."

The list of current omens and superstitions which she has unearthed may prove of interest to Western readers who have little idea of the burden of *taboo* under which the average Hindu passes his days. The essayist says:

"An attempt to enumerate these superstitious beliefs would be useless, but the following would illustrate the villagers' deep regard for them, It is a good omen to hear a bell ring, an ass bray, or a Brahmini kite cry, when starting out to see a married woman whose husband is alive. They believe it to be an excellent omen to see a corpse, a bunch of flowers, water, milk, a toddy pot, or a washerman with dirty clothes, while setting out to give any present to her or her husband. No Hindu man or woman would set out to visit a newly married couple if he or she hears sneezing while starting, or proceed on the journey if he or she hears the wailing of a beggar, or happens to see a Brahmin widow, a snake, a full oil pot, or a cat."

[Illustration: IN THE CLOISTER'S STUDIOUS SHADE]

[Illustration: MISS JACKSON AND SOME SOCIAL SERVICE WORKERS]

The College Woman and India.

Many of the students are full of ideas as to the various places which women may fill in the economy of the India of the future. Among the professions open to women, teaching is of course the favorite. Its opportunities are shown in the following:

"The University women who, more than any one else, have enjoyed the fruits of education and the privileges of college life are naturally very keen on imparting them to the million of their less graduate sisters. Almost every student in a college is now filled with a greater love and longing to help the uneducated women. Thus, most of them go out as teachers. Some of them work in their own schools, or take up work either in a mission school or a government school. Some of the graduates are now in a position to establish schools of their own. The pay for teachers is usually lower than that earned by women in other positions, but the fact that so many women become teachers shows that they care more for service than for salary, for surely this is the greatest service that they as women can give to India."

Another student has some ideas as to new methods to be used:

"The present method of teaching in India is not quite suitable to the modern stage of children. Now, children are very inquisitive and try to learn by themselves. They cannot understand anything which is taught as mere doctrines. The teacher has to draw her answers from the children and thus build up her teaching on the base of their previous knowledge. So the educated women have to train themselves in schools where they are made fit to meet the present standard of children."

Miss Cornelia Sorabji has shown by her career what a woman lawyer can do for other women. A college girl writes as follows of the opportunities for service that other students might find in the law:

"I have seen many women in the villages, though not educated, showing the capacities of a good lawyer. I think that women have a special talent in performing this business, and hence would do much better than men. Tenderness and mercy are qualities greatly required in a judge or magistrate. Women are famous for these and so their judgments which will be the products of justice tempered by mercy will be commendable. A man cannot understand so fully a woman, the workings of her mind, her thoughts and her views, as a woman can; so in order to plead the cause of women there should be women lawyers who could understand and put their cases in a very clear light."

Another feels the need of women in politics:

"According to the present system in India, the government is carried on by men alone. Thus women are exclusively shut off from the administration of the country. The good and bad results of the government affect men and women alike. Therefore, it is only fair that women also should have an active part in the government of the country. Women should be given seats in the Legislative Council where they would have an opportunity to listen to the problems of the country and try to solve them.

"From ordinary life we see that women are more economical than men. Therefore, it would be better for the country if women could take a part in economic matters. When the rate of tax is fixed men are likely to decide it merely from a consideration of their income without thinking about small expenses. Women are acquainted with every expense in detail. If women could take part in economic affairs, the expenditure of a country would be directed in a better and more careful way.

"In national and international questions also women can take a part. Women are more conservative, sympathetic, and kind than men. Great changes and misery which are not foreseen at all are brought by wars between different countries. Women, too, can consider about the affairs of wars as well as men. Their sympathetic and conservative views will help the people not to plunge into needless wars and political complications.

"Women know as well as, and perhaps more than men, the evils which result from the illiteracy of people and their unsanitary conditions. Men spend much of their time outside home, while women in their quiet homes can see their surroundings and watch the needs of people around them. So women can give good ideas in matters concerning education and sanitation. In this way, women can influence the public opinion of a place and the government of a country depends much on the nature of public opinion."

But with all these "new woman theories" the claims of home are not forgotten:

"Among the many possibilities opening out to women, we cannot fail to mention *home life*, though it is nothing new.

"According to the testimony of all history, the worth and blessing of men and nations depend in large measure on the character and ordering of family life. 'The family is the structural cell of the social organism. In it lives the power of propagation and renewal of life. It is the foundation of morality, the chief educational institution, and the source of nearly all real contentment among men.' All other questions sink into insignificance when the stability of the family is at stake. In short, the family circle is a world in miniature, with its own habits, its own interests, and its own ties, largely independent of the great world that lies outside. When the family is of such great importance, how much greater should be the responsibilities of women in the ordering of that life? Is it not there in the home that we develop most of our habits, our lines of thought and action?

"Even while keeping home, woman can do other kinds of work. She can help her husband in his varied activities by showing interest and sympathy in all that he does; she can influence him in every possible way. Then also she may do social and religious work, and even teaching, though she has to manage a home. But *the* work that needs her keenest attention is in the home itself, in training up the children. Happiness and cheerfulness in the home circle depend more or less on the radiant face of the mother, as she performs her simple tasks, upon her tenderness, on her unwearied willingness to surpass all boundaries in love. She is the 'centre' of the family. The physical and moral training of her children falls to her lot.

"Now, the developing of character is no light task, nor is it the least work that has to be done. The family exists to train individuals for membership in a large group. In the little family circle attention can be concentrated on a few who in turn can go out and influence others. The family, therefore, is the nursery of all human virtues and powers.

"In conclusion, expressing the same idea in stronger words, it is to be noted that whether India shall maintain her self-government, when she receives it, depends on how far the women are ready to fulfill the obligations laid upon them. This is a great question and has to be decided by the educated women of India."

[Illustration: In the Laboratory, Madras]

[Illustration: Tennis Champions with Cup AT WORK AND PLAY]

One Reformer and What She Achieved.

Pushpam's father is growing old; lands and jewels have shrunk. Married sons and daughters are already gathering and saving for the future of their own young daughters. Three thousand rupees are demanded of Pushpam in the marriage market. The thought of it is marring the peace of her father's face and breaking his sleep of nights. But Pushpam has news to impart, "Father, I have something to say. It will hurt you, but I must speak. It is the first time that I, your daughter, have even disobeyed your wishes, but this time it must be.

"All this college term we girls have been thinking and talking of our marriage system and its evils. Husbands are bought in the market, and in these war years they, like everything else, are high. A man thinks not of the girl who will make his home, but of the rupees she will bring to his father's coffers. Marriage means not love, but money. My classmates and I have talked and written and thought. Now three of us have made one another a solemn promise. Our parents shall give no dowries for us. We have no fear of remaining unmarried; we can earn our way as we go and find our happiness in work. Or if there are men who care for us, and not for the rupees we bring, let them ask for us; we will consider such marriages, but no other. Do not protest, Father, for our minds are made up."

[Illustration: THE NEW DORMITORY AT MADRAS COLLEGE]

The old man, for years autocrat of the village, bows to the will of his youngest child, fearing the jeers of relatives, yet unable to withstand.

No, Pushpam did not remain single. In men's colleges the same ferment is going on, and when a suitor came he said, "I want you for yourself, not for the gold that you might bring." He married Pushpam, and their joy of Christian service is not shadowed by the financial distress brought upon the father's house.

Mary Smith asked to be shown the justification of college education for Indian girls. Is it good? The College of the Sunflower has its home in dignified and seemly buildings set in a tropical garden. Does its beauty draw students away from the world of active life, or send them with fresh strength to share its struggles. Pushpam has given one answer. Another one may find in the college report of 1921 with its register of graduates. Name after name rolls out its story of busy lives—married women, who are housemakers and also servants of the public weal; government inspectresses of schools, who tour around "the district," bringing new ideas and encouragement to isolated schools; teachers and teachers, and yet more teachers, in government and mission schools, and schools under private management. Only six years of existence, and yet the Sunflower has opened so wide, the Lamp has lighted so many candles in dim corners. Will the Mary Smiths of America do their part that the next six years may be bigger and better than the last?

The spirit of Madras Students is shown in the following extracts from personal letters written to former teachers:

FROM A GRADUATE OF MADRAS CHRISTIAN COLLEGE

"Last week we had the special privilege of hearing Mr. and Mrs. Annett, of India Sunday School Union. The last day Mr. Annett showed how we can lead our children to Christ and make them accept Christ as their Master. That is the aim of religious education. My heart thrilled within me when I heard Mr. Annett in his last lecture confirm what I had thought out as principles in teaching and training the young, and I found my eyes wet. But the very faith which Jesus had in people and which triumphs over all impossibilities I am trying to have. I have patiently turned to the girls and am trying to help them in their lives. The Christ power in me is revealing to me many things since I surrendered to Him my will. He is showing me what mighty works one can do through intercessory prayer which I try to do with many failings.

"Politics have lately been very interesting to me. Rather I have been forced to enter in. You will have read or heard of the new movement in India that sprang up early in September. Gandhi is the leader. I have some clippings to send you. It is not about that I wish to write, but about the remarkable way India is repressing the movement. The Panjab, the province for which sympathy is called for and the one which affords the cause for non-co-operation, has thrown up Gandhi's scheme and her sons are standing for council elections. No Indian can help being thrilled over the nominations and elections for legislative councils and councils of state, which are to assemble in January according to the Reform Act. Our girls are taking a keen interest in the affairs of the country and earnestly praying for her.

"This is the week of prayer of the Y.W. and Y.M.C.A. I am sure you are remembering us,—the young women of India and our girls who are to lay out the future in India; also our young men and boys.

"The Student Federation has its conference in P—— during Christmas, and four of our college students are going. If only the men would be open hearted and less prejudiced and brave enough to stand alone and reform society. I think the time is coming.

"Isn't it strange that you should also feel the thirst for Bible study just as I am doing here. I never felt the lack of Scriptural knowledge as now while I teach our girls."

EXTRACTS FROM A TEACHER'S JOURNAL IN MADRAS COLLEGE

November 12, 1921.

We had nine graduates to garland last night and should have had more if Convocation had followed closely on their success in April. But now one is at Somerville College, Oxford (we have five old students in England now and one in America), one at her husband's home in Bengal, one serving in Pundita Ramabai's Widows' Home at Mukti near Poona, and three kept away by some duty in their families. Among our nine were two who had been among our very earliest students; in fact, one bears the very first name entered on our student roll in April, 1915, when we were looking round in trembling hope to see whether any students at all would entrust themselves to our inexperienced hands. These two, of course, left some years ago, but have since taken the teachers' degree, the Licentiate in Teaching, for which they have prepared themselves by private study while serving in schools.

This L.T. is a University degree open to graduates in Arts only, and a B.A., L.T., is regarded as a teacher fully equipped for the highest posts in schools. The preparation for it has been carried on hitherto chiefly at a Government Teachers' College, where the few women students, though very courteously treated, have naturally been at a great disadvantage among more than a hundred men. Such of our graduates as have spent the required year there have been considerably disappointed, feeling that their work has been too easy and too theoretical. In any case it is impossible that much practical work could be found for so large a number of students, and the belief is growing that the ideal training college is a small one. That it must be a Christian one is from our point of view still more important. The women B.A., L.T.'s will hold positions of greater influence than any other class in South India. They will be Government Inspectresses, Heads of

Middle Schools and High Schools, lecturers in Training Colleges, in fact, the sources of the inspiration which will permeate every region of women's education. Before long the missions will be unable to keep pace with the rapid increase of available pupils for girls' schools. Their success in originating and fostering the idea of educating girls has now produced a situation with which we cannot personally cope, but which we can indirectly control by concentrating effort at the most vital spot, that is the training of the highest rank of women teachers. These will set the tone and, to a great extent, determine the quality of the women teachers who have lower qualifications, and these will have in their hands the training of ever-increasing numbers of girl pupils and will hand on the ideals which they have themselves received. It was an honor which we felt very deeply when the Missionary Educational Council of South India entrusted to the council of our College the task of inaugurating an L.T. College for Women, and we have been very busy about it.

December 15, 1921.

More than a month has passed since I began the Journal and I am now sitting in the junior B.A. class-room watching over nineteen students (the twentieth happens to be absent) who are writing their terminal examination papers. I was a false weather-prophet; rain did not come, and still keeps away. Instead there is a high cool wind, and every one of these students is firmly holding down her paper with the left hand while her fountain pen (they all have fountain pens) skims all too rapidly over the page. The great principle of answering an examination paper is never to waste a moment on thought. If you do not know what to say next, repeat what you said before until a new idea strikes you. As it is not necessary to dip the pen in ink it should never leave the page. This method enables them to produce small pamphlets which they hand in with a happy sense of achievement, but the examiner's heart sinks as she gathers up the volumes of hasty manuscript.

Sometimes, however, the answers err on the side of conciseness. "We believe them because we cannot prove them," was the truthful reply of a student in Physics to the question, "Why do we believe Newton's Laws of Motion?" Or sometimes an essential transition is omitted; "At the period of the Roman conquest the Greeks were politically hopeless, economically bankrupt, and morally corrupt. They became teachers." But sometimes it is the caprice of the English language which betrays them. "The events of the 15th century which most affected philosophic thought were the founding of America and the founding of the Universe." Occasionally they administer an unconscious rebuke. I was just starting out to give an address at a week-night evening service from the chancel steps of a neighboring church, and having a minute or two to spare I took up one of my 120 Scripture papers and read, "St. Paul's chief difficulty with the Corinthians was that women insisted on speaking in church. It is wicked for women to talk in church."

The nineteen students before me are very representative of our student body, which now numbers one hundred and thirty. Eleven are writing on Constitutional History, two on Philosophy, four on Zoology and two (a young Hindu married girl and a Syrian Christian) on Malayalam literature. Ten of them speak Tamil, eight Malayalam, and one Telugu. They vary in rank from high official circles to very low origins, but most belong to what we should call the professional classes. All are barefooted and wear the Indian dress, which in the case of the Syrians is always white.

Through the open door I look into the library where the fifty-three new students of this year are writing an English paper. There are eight Hindus and one European among them, also two students from Ceylon, two from Hyderabad, and one, differing widely from the rest in dress and facial type, from Burma. The lecturer in charge is Miss Chamberlain, the daughter of our invaluable secretary in America. She arrived only three weeks ago to take the place of Miss Sarber who has started on her furlough and already the dignity of the philosopher and psychologist is mingling with the gaiety which makes her table a favorite place for students.

The debate on the conscience clause[*] which took place in the new Legislative Assembly in November shows that the party now in power, the non-Brahmin middle-class, realizes the value to the country of Christian education. Man after man rose to express his gratitude to the Christian College and to point out that missionaries alone had brought education to low-caste and out-caste people. The proposal was rejected by 61 votes to 13, a most unexpected and happy event.

One proposal, perfectly well meant, was made at the Government Committee on Education which aroused great indignation among our students. It was that various concessions should be made to the supposed weakness of women students and that the pass mark in examinations should be lowered for them. As the Principals of both the Women's Colleges opposed the suggestion, it was withdrawn, but this little incident shows two things, the sympathetic feeling of men toward the studies of women, and the distance that women have travelled since the time when they would themselves have requested such concessions.

In the recent agitation in favor of Nationalism finding that the only constructive advice given was to devote themselves to Indian music, to the spinning wheel, which is Mr. Gandhi's great remedy for social and political ills and to social service, I did all that I could to promote these ends. I asked the Senior Student to collect the names of all who wished to learn to play an Indian instrument, I presented the College with a pound of raw cotton and spinning wheel of the type recommended by Mr. Gandhi, and the social service begun some months before was continued This last consists of our expedition led by Miss Jackson, which twice a week visits an unpleasant little village not far from our gates. The students wash the children, which is not at all a delightful task, attend to sore eyes and matted hair and teach them games and songs, and chat with the village women about household hygiene and how to keep out of debt. One of our Sunday Schools is in this village, too, so by this time the students are welcome visitors, and whether they do much good or not, they learn a great deal of sobering truth. Of course, only a few can go at a time, but others find some scope in the other Sunday Schools and in the little Day School which Miss Brockway instituted for the children of our servants. This last means real self-denial, as the work must be done every day. Still, it remains one of our greatest problems to find channels for the spirit of service which we try to inspire, and without which the current of their patriotism may become stagnant.

But I am being disappointed about the music and the spinning wheel. Not one student was willing to undergo the toilsome practice of learning an instrument, and though the spinning wheel was received with enthusiasm the pound of cotton has hardly diminished at all. Nor will they take the trouble to read the newspapers regularly. So that they might not feel that too British a view of events was presented to them they are supplied with some papers of a very critical tone, but I need not have feared the risk, the papers remain unread. They much prefer the medium of speech, and are keenly interested in almost any topic on which we invite an attractive speaker to give an address, but they do not follow it up by reading. They are decidedly fonder of books than they were, and use the library more, but their taste is for the better kind of domestic fiction more than for anything else. There is one important exception, they all love Shakespeare and there is no one whom they so delight to act. Whenever they invite us to an entertainment, which they do on many and various occasions, we are fairly sure of seeing a few scenes of Shakespeare acted much better than I have ever seen English girls of their age act.

The students have been collecting a fund for our new Science building, a great and beautiful enterprise, which, also, is still in its proper stage. The drawing of plans so large and detailed has occupied many months. We are looking to America for the generous gift which shall bring these plans into actuality, but help from other sources is welcome, too, and particularly help from the students. They have made many efforts and reached a sum of more than Rs. 500. Their most important undertaking was a performance of "Everyman" most solemnly and beautifully carried out before an audience of our women friends, and there was also a dramatic version written by one of the students of the parable of the prodigal son and performed before the college only. This last was remarkable in its adaptation of the story to Indian conditions and for the characteristic introduction of a mother and a sister.

[Illustration: THE OLD INDIA
No Chance—No Hope]

> "If she have sent her servants in our pain,
> If she have fought with Death and dulled his sword,
> If she have given back our sick again
> And to the breast the weakling lips restored,
> Is it a little thing that she has wrought?
> Then Life and Death and Motherhood be nought."

Kipling's "Song of the Women"

The Medical School at Vellore is still without a permanent home and is lodged in scattered buildings—without a permanent staff except for two or three heroic figures who are performing each the work of several—without a certainty of a regular income in any way equivalent to its needs—but it has an enthusiastic band of students and it has Dr. Ida Scudder, and so the balance is on the right side.

[Footnote *: Opposing the study of the Bible in our schools.]

CHAPTER FIVE

SENT FORTH TO HEAL

"THE Long Trail A-Winding."

Who that has read "Kim" will ever forget Kipling's picture of the Grand Trunk Road, with its endless panorama of beggars, Brahmans, Lamas, and talkative old women on pilgrimage? Such roads cover India's plains with a network of interlacing lines, for one of Britain's achievements on India's behalf has been her system of metalled roads, defying alike the dust of the dry season and the floods of the monsoon.

One such road I have in mind, a road leading from the old fortress town of Vellore through twenty-three miles of fertile plain, to Gudiyattam, at the foot of the Eastern Ghats. It is just a South Indian "up country" road, skirting miles of irrigated rice fields, gold-green in their beginnings, gold-brown in the days of ripening and reaping. It winds past patches of sugar cane and cocoanut palm; then half arid uplands, where goats and lean cattle search for grass blades that their predecessors have overlooked; then the *bizarre* shapes of the ghats, wide spaces open to the play of sun and wind and rain, of passing shadow and sunset glory. They are among the breathing spaces of earth, which no man hath tamed or can tame.

An Indian "Flivver."

An ordinary road it is, and passing over it the ordinary procession—heavy-wheeled carts drawn by humped, white bullocks; crowded jutkas whose tough, little ponies disappear in a rattle of wheels and a cloud of dust; weddings, funerals, and festivals with processions gay or mournful as the case may be. One feature alone distinguishes this road from others of its kind; once a week its dusty length is traversed by a visitant from the West, a "Tin Lizzie," whose unoccupied spaces are piled high with medicine chests and instrument cases. Once a week the Doctor passes by, and the countryside turns out to meet her.

When the Doctor Passes by.

Where do they come from, the pathetic groups that continually bring the little Ford to a halt? For long stretches the road passes through apparently uninhabited country, yet here they are, the lame, the halt, and the blind, as though an unseen city were pouring out the dregs of its slums. Back a mile from the road, among the tamarind trees, stands one village; at the edge of the rice fields huddles another. The roofs of thatch or earth-brown tiles seem an indistinguishable part of the landscape, but they are there, each with its quota of child-birth pain, its fever-burnings, its germ-borne epidemics where sanitation is unknown, its final pangs of dissolution. But once a week the Doctor passes by.

What do she and her attendants treat? Sore eyes and scabies and all the dirt-carried minor ailments that infect the village; malaria from the mosquitoes that swarm among the rice fields; aching teeth to be pulled; dreaded epidemics of cholera or typhoid, small pox or plague. Now and then the back seat is cleared of its *impedimenta* and turned into the fraction of an ambulance to convey a groaning patient to a clean bed in the hospital ward. Once at least a makeshift operating table has been set up under the shade of a roadside banyan tree, and the Scriptural injunction, "If thy foot offend thee, cut it off," carried out then and there to the saving of a life.

At dark the plucky little Ford plods gallantly back to the home base, its occupants with faded garlands, whose make-up varies with the seasons— yellow chrysanthemums with purple everlasting tassels at Christmas time; in the dry, hot days of spring pink and white oleanders from the water channels among the hills; during the rains the heavy fragrance of jasmine. All the flowers do their brave best for the day when the Doctor passes by.

Where no Doctor Passes by.

But what of the roads on which the Doctor never passes? From Vellore's fortress-crowned hills they stretch north and south, east and west, and toward all the intermediate points of the compass. Every city of India forms such a nucleus for the country around. Amid the wheat fields of the Punjab, under the tamarinds of the Ganges plain, among the lotus pools and bamboo clusters of the Bengal deltas, and on the black cotton fields of the Deccan are the roads and the villages, the villages and the roads. Some mathematically minded writer once computed that, if Christ in the days of His flesh had started on a tour among the villages of India, visiting one each day, to-day in the advancing years of the twentieth century many would yet be waiting, unenlightened and unvisited. Few have been visited by any modern follower of the Great Physician. Who can compute their sum total of human misery, of preventable disease, of undernourishment, of pain that might all too easily he alleviated?

[Illustration: Kamala (Lotus Flower), Winner of The Gold Medal in Anatomy in Vellore Medical School]

[Illustration: A Little Lost One—What Will Such Girls Do for India? CONTRASTS]

A Problem In Multiplication.

Was it, one wonders, the memory of the Gudiyattam road, and those like it in nameless thousands, that burned deep into Dr. Ida Scudder's heart and brain the desire to found a Medical School, where the American Doctor might multiply herself and reproduce her life of skillful and devoted service in the lives of hundreds of Indian women physicians? It is the only way that the message of the Good Physician, His healing for soul and body, may penetrate those village fastnesses of dirt, disease, and ignorance. One hundred and sixty women doctors at present try to minister to India's one hundred and sixty millions of women, shut out by immemorial custom from men's hospitals and from physicians who are men. "What are these among so many?" What can they ever be except as they may multiply themselves in the persons of Indian messengers of healing?

Small Beginnings.

And so, in July, 1918, the Vellore Medical School was opened, under the fostering care of four contributing Mission Boards, and with the approval and aid of the Government of Madras. "Go ahead if you can find six students who have completed the High School Course," said the interested Surgeon General. Instead of six, sixty-nine applied; seventeen were accepted; and fourteen not only survived the inevitable weeding out process, but brought to the school at the end of the first year the unheard of distinction of one hundred per cent. of passes in the Government examination. That famous first class is now in its Senior Year, and by the time this book comes from the press will be scattering itself among thirteen centres of help and health.

And so, in rented buildings, the Medical School started life. If ever an institution passed its first year in a hand-to-mouth existence, this one has. Short of funds save as mercifully provided by private means; short of doctors for the staff; short of buildings in which to house its increasing student body, for it has grown from fourteen to sixty-seven; short, in fine, of everything needed except faith and enthusiasm and hard work on the part of its founders, it has yet gone on; the girls have been housed, classes have been taught, examinations passed, and the first class is ready to go out into the world of work.

Just here perhaps one brief explanation should be made. These girls will not be *doctors* in the narrowly technical sense, for the Government of India reserves the doctor's degree for such students as have first taken a college diploma and then on top of it a still more demanding medical course of five years. These students will receive the degree of Licensed Medical Practitioner (L.M.P.) which authorizes them to practise medicine and surgery and even to be in charge of a hospital. The full college may come, we hope, not many years hence, when funds become available. Meantime, this school will year by year be turning out its quota of medical workers whose usefulness cannot be over-estimated.

[Illustration: FIRST BUILDING AT NEW MEDICAL SCHOOL, VELLORE, WHICH IS
HOUSING OUR STUDENTS]

A Visit to Vellore.

Let us pay a visit to the School and see it as it is in its present state of makeshift. Since its beginning it has dwelt, like Paul the prisoner, "in its own hired house," but Paul's epistles tell of no such uncertainty in his tenure of his rented dwelling, as that which has afflicted this institution. The housing shortage which has distressed New York has reached even to Vellore. Two rented bungalows were lost, and, as an emergency measure, the future Nurses' Home was erected in great haste on the town site and at once utilized as a dormitory with some rooms set aside for lectures as well.

Corpses—and Children.

Let us first pay a visit to "Pentland," the one remaining "hired house," in which the Freshmen have their home with Dr. Mary Samuel, the Indian member of the staff, as their house mother. Just behind it is the thatched shed, carefully walled in, which serves as the dissecting room. To the uninitiated it is a place of gruesome smells and sights, for cadavers, whole or in fragments, litter the tables. The casual visitor sympathizes with the Hindu student who confides to you that during her first days of work in the dissecting room she could only sleep when firmly flanked by a friend on each side of her "to keep off the spirits that walk by night." After a few weeks of experience, however, the fascinating search for nerve and muscle, tendon, vein, and artery becomes the dominating state of consciousness, and the scientific spirit excludes all resentment at the disagreeable.

Pentland Compound possesses another feature in pleasing contrast to the dissecting shed. As you come away from a session there and close the door of the enclosing wall, from the opposite end of the compound comes the sound of children's voices in play. There in a comfortable Indian cottage lives the jolly family of the Children's Home. They are a merry, well-nourished collection of waifs and strays, of all ancestries, Hindu, Muhammadan, and Christian, mostly gathered in through the wards of the Mission Hospitals. Only an experienced social worker could estimate what such a home means in the prevention of future disease, beggary, and crime. It is good for the medical students to live in close neighborliness with this bit of actual service. One student in writing of her future plans mentions that, as an "avocation" in the chinks of her hospital work, she plans to raise private funds and found a little orphanage all her own!

Early Rising.

Not far from Pentland are the new buildings of Voorhees College belonging to the Arcot Mission of the Dutch Reformed Church. For the resent, the Medical School has the loan of its lecture rooms and laboratories in the early morning hours before the boys' classes begin. That means seven o'clock classes, and previous to that for most of the students a mile walk from the town dormitory. Here is the Chemistry Laboratory. Freshmen toil over the puzzling behavior of atoms and electrons, while in lecture rooms the ear of the uninstructed visitor is puzzled by the technical vocabularies of the classes in anatomy and surgery, and one wonders how the Indian student ever achieves this vast amount of information through the difficult medium of a foreign tongue.

[Illustration: DR. SCUDDER AND THE MEDICAL STUDENTS AT VELLORE.]

In Hospital Wards.

Next in our path of visitation comes Schell Hospital, where the theories learned in dissecting room, laboratory, and lecture are connected up with actual relief of sick women and children. Here the students are divided into small groups and many kinds of clinical demonstrations are going on at once. In the compounding room you will see a lesson in pill-making. That smiling young person working away on the floor in front of the table is a West Coast Brahman, sent on a stipend from the Hindu state of Travancore. It is her first experience away from home and the zest and adventure of the new life have already fired her spirit.

In this verandah another group are at work with bandaging. We watch them while brown arms and legs, heads and bodies disappear under complicated layers of white gauze.

In the large ward Seniors, equipped with head mirrors and stethoscopes, with chart and pen, are taking down patients' histories and suggesting diagnoses. Soon it will be their work to do this unaided, and every bit of supervised practice is laying up stores of experience for the future.

On the next verandah Doctor Findlay is giving a lecture and demonstration on the care and feeding of babies. Demonstration is not difficult, for the hospital always provides an abundance of ailing infants whose regulated diet and consequently improving health serve as laboratory tests.

The Ford in a New Capacity.

Now we follow the shady verandah around three sides of the attractive courtyard with its trees and flowering creepers. At the far end the class in obstetrics is going on. And behold, the irrepressible Ford has entered into a new province. This truly American product will probably be found to-day in every continent and nearly every country in the world, but one ventures to prophesy that Vellore is the only spot on the habitable globe where its cast-off tires have been metamorphosed into models of human organs! Every student not working over an actual mother or baby is busy performing on these home-made rubber models the operations she may some day be called to do upon a living patient.

In the midst of these Dr. Griscom is interrupted by next ward that didn't cry for a week? You know that this morning you slapped it and it cried for the first time, and its mother was very happy. Now she wants to hear it cry again, and says—"may she please beat it herself?" The Doctor leaves her Ford tires, and runs to the ward to explain to the overzealous mother the difference between *massage* administered by a physician and the ordinary manner of "beating" a baby.

[Illustration: Interior of the Temple Where God is a Stone Image]

[Illustration: Interior of the Hospital Where God is Love]

Our next place of pilgrimage is the "town site" where the new Nurses' Home affords temporary dormitory accommodation. Beside it is the Doctor's bungalow, and in the open space next is to be built the big dispensary. This is well called the "town site," for it is in the thick of Vellore's population. Children, dogs, and donkeys swarm across its precincts, and there is no fear of these students being separated from the actualities of Indian life. The two-story buildings, however, give abundant opportunity for the occupants to "lift up their eyes unto the hills"; and the open air sleeping-rooms promise breezes in the hottest nights.

"Mrs. Earth Thou-Art."

Here, too, the Seniors have their lectures in obstetrics, and with the beginning of that course a new difficulty arose. Equipment here, as in practically every Mission institution, is pitifully limited by lack of funds. For the proper teaching of obstetrics there is need of a pelvic manikin, lifesize. There were no funds to spare for so expensive a piece of apparatus, and, if there had been, there would have been a delay of months in getting it out from England or America. But meantime obstetrics must be taught, and a manikin must be had. "Necessity is the mother of invention." Necessity got to work, and "Mrs. Earth-Thou-Art" is the result. Dr. Griscom sent for the potter, who left his wheel in the bazaar and came to this market for new wares. After long and detailed instructions, he returned to his wheel, and set it to the making of a shape never seen in the potter's vision of Jeremiah or Robert Browning. The first attempt was a failure; the second and third were equally useless; at last something was produced that approximated the human size and form. The tires of the Ford were again requisitioned and, by the miraculous aid of the blacksmith, nailed to the pottery figure without wrecking the latter. "Mrs. Earth-Thou-Art" at last reposed complete, one example of the triumph of the missionary teacher over the handicaps of the situation. We hope that her brittle clay will survive until such time as some friend from across the sea is moved to provide for her a "store-made" successor.

"That which shall be."

One more spot must be visited before our pilgrimage ends. No guest of the Medical School is ever allowed to depart without a visit to "the site," that pride of Dr. Ida Scudder and her staff.

Three miles out from the dust and noise of the bazaars lies this tract of fertile land, the near hills rising even within its boundaries, the heights of Kylasa forming a mountain wall against the sunset. Here in the midst of natural beauty, open to every wind of heaven, the dormitories, lecture room, chapel, and new hospital will rise. It will mean a healthful home, with the freedom of country life and endless opportunity for games and walks. The motor ambulances will form the daily connecting link with the practical work of dispensary and emergency hospital.

"Who's Who."

We have spoken much of buildings and courses of study, but little of the girls themselves. Who are they? Where do they come from? Why are they here? What are their future plans?

They are girls of many shades of belief, from many classes of society. The great majority are, of course, Protestant Christians, representing the work of almost every Mission Board to be found in South India. There are a few Roman Catholics, and about an equal number of members of the indigenous Syrian Christian community. Nine are Hindus, including one Brahman. They come from the remotest corners of the Madras Presidency, and some from even beyond its borders.

Why did they come? There are some who frankly admit that their entrance into Medical School was due solely to the influence of parents and relatives, and that their present vital interest in what they are doing dates back not to any childhood desire for the doctor's profession, but only to the stimulating experiences of the school itself. Others tell of a life-long wish for what the school has made possible; still others of "sudden conversion" to medicine, brought about by a realization of need, or in one case to the chance advice of a school friend. Two speak of the appalling need of their own home villages, where no medical help for women has ever been known. Some of the students have expressed their reasons in their own words:—

"Once I had a severe attack of influenza and was taken to the General Hospital, Madras. I have heard people say that nurses and doctors are not good to the patients. But, contrary to my idea, the English and Eurasian nurses there were very good and kind to me, more than I expected. I used to see the students of the Medical College of Madras paying visits to all the patients, some of whom were waiting for mornings when they should meet their medical friends. I saw all the work that they did. The nurses were very busy helping patients and, whatever trouble the patients gave, they never got cross with them. They used to sing to some of them at night, give toys to little ones and thus coax every one to make them take medicine. I admired the kindness and goodness that all the medical workers with whom I came in contact possessed. As medical work began to interest me, I used to read magazines about medical work. Again, when I once went to Karimnagar, I saw ever so many children and women, uncared for and not being loved by high caste people. I wanted to help Indians very much. All these things made me join the Medical School.

"My father's desire was that one of his daughters should study medicine and work in the hospital where he worked for twenty years, and so in order to fulfill his desire I made up my mind to learn medicine.

"Now my father is dead and the hospital in which he had worked is closed, for there is no one to take his place. So all are very glad to see that I am learning medicine. There are many men doctors in Ceylon, but very few lady doctors and I think that God has given me a good opportunity to work for Him.

"For a long time I did not know much about the sufferings of my country women without proper aid of medical women. One day I happened to attend a meeting held by some Indian ladies and one European. They spoke about the great need of women doctors in India and all about the sufferings of my sisters. One fact struck me more than anything else. It was about an untrained mid-wife who treated a woman very cruelly, but ignorantly. From that time I made up my mind to study medicine with the aim of becoming a loving doctor. My wish is now that all the women doctors should be real Christian doctors with real love and sympathizing hearts for the patients.

"When I told my parents that I wanted to study medicine, they and my relatives objected and scolded me, for they were afraid that I would not marry if I would study medicine. In India they think meanly of a person, especially a girl, who is not married at the proper age. I want now to show my people that it is not mean to remain unmarried. This is my second aim which came from the first."

[Illustration: A MEDICAL STUDENT IN VELLORE]

The following is written by a Hindu student:—

"Before entering into the subject, I should like to write a few words about myself. I am the first member of our community to attain English education. Almost all my relatives (I talk only about the female members of our community) have learnt only to write and read our mother language Telugu.

"When I entered the high school course I had a poor ambition to study medicine. I do not know whether it was due to the influence of my brother-in-law who is a doctor, or whether it was due to our environments. Near our house was a small hospital. It was doing excellent work for the last five years. Now unfortunately the hospital has been closed for want of stock and good doctors. From that hospital I learnt many things. I was very intimate with the doctors. I admired the work they were doing.

"My father had a faithful friend. He was a Brahman. He realized from his own experience the want of lady doctors. He had a daughter, his only child, and she died for want of proper medical aid. Whenever my father's friend used to see me he used to ask my father to send me to the Medical College, for he was quite interested in me, like my own father. After all, as soon as I passed the School Final Examination, it was decided that I should take up medicine, but at that time my mother raised many an objection, saying the caste rules forbid it. I left the idea with no hope of renewing it and joined the Arts College. I studied one year in the College. Then luckily for me my father and his friend tried for a scholarship.

"Luckily again, it was granted by the Travancore Government.

"I am not going to close before I tell a few words of my short experience in the College. As soon as I came here I thought I wouldn't be able to learn all the things I saw here. I looked upon everything with strange eyes and everything seemed strange to me, too. But, as the days passed, I liked all that was going on in the College. The study—I now long to hear more of it and study it. Now everything is going on well with me and I hope to realize my ambition with the grace of the Almighty, for the 'thoughts of wise men are Heaven-gleams.'"

[Illustration: BETTER BABIES Throughout India. Feeding and Weighing]

You ask, what of the future? What will these young doctors bring to India's need? How much will they *do*? Might one dare to prophesy that in years to come they will at least in their own localities make stories like the following impossible?

A woman still young, though mother of seven living children, is carried into the maternity ward of the Woman's Hospital. At the hands of the ignorant mid-wife she has suffered maltreatment whose details cannot be put into print, followed by a journey in a springless cart over miles of rutted country road. She is laid upon the operating table with the blessed aid of anaesthetics at hand; there is still time to save the baby. But what of the mother? Only one more case of "too late." Pulseless, yet perfectly conscious, she hears the permission given to the relatives to take her home, and knows all too well what those words mean. The Hospital has saved her baby; her it cannot save. Clinging to the doctor's hand she cries:

"Oh, Amma, I am frightened. Why do you send me away? I must live. My little children,—this is the eighth. I don't care for myself, but I must live for them. Who will care for them if I am gone? Oh, let me live!"

And the doctor could only answer, "Too late."

On that road where the doctor passes by, one day she saw a beautiful boy of one year, "the only son of his mother." The eyelids were shut and swollen. "His history?" the doctor asks. Ordinary country sore eyes that someway refused to get well; a journey through dust and heat to a distant shrine of healing; numberless circlings of the temple according to orthodox Hindu rites; then a return home to order from the village jeweller two solid silver eyeballs as offerings to the deity of the shrine. Weeks are consumed by these doings, for in sickness as in health the East moves slowly. Meantime the eyes are growing more swollen, more painful. At last someone speaks of the weekly visit of the doctor on the Gudiyattam Road.

The doctor picked up the baby, pushed back the swollen eyelids, and washed away the masses of pus, only to find both eyeballs utterly destroyed. One more to be added to the army of India's blind! One more case of "too late"! One more atom in the mass of India's unnecessary, preventable suffering,—that suffering which moved to compassion the heart of the Christ. How many more weary generations must pass before we, His followers, make such incidents impossible? How many before Indian women with pitying eyes and tender hands shall have carried the gift of healing, the better gift of the health that outstrips disease, through the roads and villages of India?

[Illustration: Freshman Class at Vellore]

[Illustration: Latest Arrivals at Vellore]

The existence of the Medical School has been made possible by the gifts of American women. Its continued existence and future growth depend upon the same source. Gifts in this case mean not only money, but life. Where are those American students who are to provide the future doctors and nurses not only to "carry on" this school as it exists, but to build it up into a great future? It is to the girls now in high school and college that the challenge of the future comes. Among the conflicting cries of the street and market place, comes the clear call of Him whom we acknowledge as Master of life, re-iterating the simple words at the Lake of Galilee, "What is that to thee? Follow thou me."

Rupert Brooke has sung of the summons of the World War that cleansed the heart from many pettinesses. His words apply equally well to this service of human need which has been called "war's moral equivalent."

> "Now, God be thanked, Who has matched us with His hour,
> And caught our youth, and wakened us from sleeping,
> With hand made sure, clear eye, and sharpened power,
> To turn, as swimmers into cleanness leaping,
> Glad from a world grown old and cold and weary."

AN EXAMPLE OF CHRISTIAN TREATMENT

Volumes might be written on the atrocities and absurdities of wizards, quack doctors, and the hideous usages of native midwifery. The ministry of Christian physicians comes as a revelation to the tortured victims.

The scene is a ward in a Christian Hospital for women in South India. The patients in adjacent beds, convalescents, converse together.

"What's the matter with you?" says Bed No. 1 contentedly. "My husband became angry with me, because the meal wasn't ready when he came home and he cut my face. The Doctor Miss Sahib has mended me, she has done what my own mother would not do." Said another in reply to the question, "The cow horned my arm, but until I got pneumonia I couldn't stop milking or making bread for the father of my children, even if it was broken. The hospital is my Mabap (mother-father)."

"What care would you get at home?" chimed in another who had been burning up with fever. "Oh! I would be out in the deserted part of the woman's quarters. It would be a wonderful thing if any one would pass me a cup of water," she replied. From another bed, a young wife of sixteen spoke of having been ill with abscesses. "One broiling day," she said, "I had fainted with thirst. The midwives had neglected me all through the night, and, thinking I was dying, they threw me from the cord-bed to the floor, and dragged me down the steep stone staircase to the lowest cellar where I was lying, next to the evil-smelling dust-bin, ready for removal by the carriers of the dead, when the Doctor Miss Sahib found me and brought me here. She is my mother and I am her child."

An old woman in Bed No. 4 exhorts the patients around her to trust the mission workers. "I was against them once," she tells them, "but now I know what love means. Caste? What is caste? I believe in the goodness they show. That is their caste."

Words profoundly wise!

On the slope of the desolate river among the tall grasses I asked her, "Maiden, where do you go shading your lamp with your mantle? My house is all dark and lonesome,—lend me your light!" She raised her dark eyes for a moment and looked at my face through the dusk. "I have come to the river," she said, "to float my lamp on the stream when the daylight wanes in the west." I stood alone among tall grasses and watched the timid flame of her lamp uselessly drifting in the tide.

In the silence of the gathering night I asked her, "Maiden, your lights are all lit—then where do you go with your lamp? My house is all dark and lonesome,—lend me your light." She raised her dark eyes on my face and stood for a moment doubtful. "I have come," she said at last, "to dedicate my lamp to the sky." I stood and watched her light uselessly burning in the void.

In the moonless gloom of midnight I asked her, "Maiden, what is your quest holding the lamp near your heart? My house is all dark and lonesome, —lend me your light." She stopped for a minute and thought and gazed at my face in the dark. "I have brought my light," she said, "to join the carnival of lamps." I stood and watched her little lamp uselessly lost among lights.

Rabindranath Tagore.

CHAPTER SIX

WOMEN WHO DO THINGS

India has boasted certain eminent women whom America knows well. Ramabai with her work for widows is a household word in American homes and colleges; President Harrison's sentences of appreciation emphasized the distinction that already belonged to Lilavati Singh; Chandra Lela's search for God has passed into literature. The Sorabji sisters are known in the worlds of law, education, and medicine.

But these names are not the only ones that India has to offer. In the streets of her great cities where two civilizations clash; in sleepy, old-world towns where men and women, born under the shade of temple towers and decaying palaces, are awakening to think new thoughts; in isolated villages where life still harks back to pre-historic days—against all these backgrounds you may find the Christian educated woman of New India measuring her untried strength against the powers of age-old tradition.

In this chapter I would tell you of a few such women whom I have met. They are not the only ones; they may not be even pre-eminent. Many who knew India well would match them with lists from other localities and in other lines of service.

These five are all college women. One had but two years in a Mission College whose course of study went no further; one carries an American degree; three are graduates of a Government College for men. All go back to the pioneer days before Madras Women's Christian College and Vellore Medical School saw the light, and when Isabella Thoburn's college department was small; all five bear proudly the name of Christian; through five different professions they are giving to the world of India their own expression of what Christianity has meant to them.

[Illustration: MRS. PAUL APPASAMY]

Home Making and Church Work.

Throughout India there exists a group of women workers, widely scattered, largely unknown to one another, in the public eye unhonored and unsung, yet performing tasks of great significance. Wherever an Indian Church raises its tower to the sky, there working beside the pastor you will find the pastor's wife.

Sometimes she lives in the heart of the Hindu town; sometimes in a village, in the primitive surroundings of a mass-movement community. Eminent among such is Mrs. Azariah, wife of the first Indian bishop, and with him at the head of the Tinnevelly Missionary Society at Dornakal. There, in the heart of the Deccan, among primitive Telugu outcastes, is this remarkable group of Indian missionaries, supported by Indian funds, winning these lowly people through the gospel of future salvation and of present betterment.

It was on a Sunday morning that I slipped into the communion service at Dornakal. The little church, built from Indian gifts with no aid from the West, is simplicity itself. The roof thatched with millet stalks, the low-hanging palmyra rafters hung with purple everlastings, the earth-floor covered with bamboo matting, all proclaimed that here was a church built and adorned by the hands of its worshippers. The Bishop in his vestments dispensed the sacrament from the simple altar. Even the Episcopal service had been so adapted to Indian conditions that instead of the sound of the expected chants one heard the Te Deum and the Venite set to the strains of Telugu lyrics. The audience, largely of teachers, theological students, and schoolboys and girls, sat on the clean floor space. One saw and listened with appreciation and reverence, finding here a beginning and prophecy of what the Christianized fraction of India will do for its motherland.

It was against this background that I came to know Mrs. Azariah. In the bungalow, as the Bishop's wife, she presides with dignity over a household where rules of plain living and high thinking prevail. She dispenses hospitality to the many European guests who come to see the activities of this experimental mission station, and packs the Bishop off well provided with food and traveling comforts for his long and numerous journeys. The one little son left at home is his mother's constant companion and shows that his training has not been neglected for the multitude of outside duties. One longs to see the house when the five older children turn homeward from school and college, and fill the bungalow with the fun of their shared experiences. Mercy, the eldest daughter, is one of the first Indian women students to venture on the new commercial course offered by the Young Women's Christian Association with the purpose of fitting herself to be her father's secretary. In a few months she will be bringing the traditions of the Women's Christian College of Madras, where she spent two previous years, to share with the Dornakal community.

But, though wife and mother and home maker, Mrs. Azariah's interests extend far beyond the confines of her family. She is president of the Madras Mothers' Union, and editor of the little magazine that travels to the homes of Tamil and Telugu Christian women, their only substitute for the "Ladies' Home Journal" and "Modern Priscilla." She is also the teacher of the women's class, made up of the wives of the theological students. A Tamil woman in a Telugu country, she, too, must have known a little of the linguistic woes of the foreign missionary. Those days, however, are long past, and she now teaches her daily classes in fluent and easy Telugu. There are also weekly trips to nearby hamlets, where the women-students are guided by her into the ways of adapting the Christian's good news to the comprehension of the plain village woman, whose interests are bounded by her house, her children, her goats, and her patch of millet.

Such a village we visited that same Sunday, when toward evening the Bishop, Mrs. Azariah, and I set out to walk around the Dornakal domain. We saw the gardens and farm from which the boys supply the whole school family with grain and fresh vegetables; we looked up to the grazing grounds and saw the herd of draught bullocks coming into the home sheds from their Sunday rest in pasture. I was told about the other activities which I should see on the working day to follow—spinning and weaving and sewing, cooking and carpentry and writing and reading—a simple Christian communism in which the boys farm and weave for the girls, and the girls cook and sew for the boys, and all live together a life that is leading up to homes of the future.

It was after all that that we saw the village. On the edge of the Mission property we came to the small group of huts, wattled from tree branches and clay, inhabited by Indian gypsy folk, just settling from nomadism into agricultural life. So primitive are they still, that lamp light is *taboo* among them, and the introduction of a kerosene lantern would force them to tear down those attempts at house architecture and move on to a fresh site, safe from the perils of civilization. It is among such primitive folk that Mrs. Azariah and her students carry their message. Herself a college woman, what experiment in sociology could be more thrilling than her contact with such a remnant of the primitive folk of the early world?

Mother, home-maker, editor, teacher, evangelist, with quiet unconsciousness and utter simplicity she is building her corner of Christian India.

Public Service.

"To-morrow is the day of the Annual Fair and I am so busy with arrangements that I had no time even to answer the note you sent me yesterday." No, this was not said in New York or Boston, but in Madras; and the speaker was not an American woman, but Mrs. Paul Appasamy, the All-India Women's Secretary of the National Missionary Society.

[Illustration: MRS. PAUL APPASAMY]

It was at luncheon time that I found Mrs. Appasamy at home, and persuaded her by shortening her meal a bit to find time to sit down with me a few minutes and tell me of some of the opportunities that Madras offers to an Indian Christian woman with a desire for service.

For such service Mrs. Appasamy has unusual qualifications. The fifth woman to enter the Presidency College of Madras, she was one of those early pioneers of woman's education, of whom we have spoken with admiring appreciation. Two years of association with Pandita Ramabai in her great work at Poona added practical experience and a familiarity with organization. Some years after her marriage to Mr. Appasamy, a barrister-at-law in Madras, came the opportunity for a year of foreign travel, divided between England and America. Such experiences could not fail to give a widened outlook, and, when Mrs. Appasamy returned to make her home in Madras, she soon found that not even with four children to look after, could her interests be confined to the walls of her own home.

American girls might be interested to know how wide a range of activities Indian life affords—how far the Western genius for organization and committee-life has invaded the East. Here is a partial list of Mrs. Appasamy's affiliations:

Member of Council and Executive for the Women's Christian College.

Vice President of the Madras Y.W.C.A.

Member of the Hostel Committee of the Y.W.C.A.

Member of the Vernacular Council of the Y.W.C.A.

Women's Secretary for All India of the National Missionary Society.

Supervisor of a Social Service Committee for Madras.

President of the Christian Service Union.

Of all her activities, Mrs. Appasamy's connection with the National Missionary Society is perhaps the most interesting. The "N.M.S.," as it is familiarly called, is a cause very near to the hearts of most Indian Christians. The work in Dornakal represents the effort of Tinnevelly Tamil Christians for the evangelization of one section of the Telugu country. The N.M.S. is a co-ordinated enterprise, taking in the contributions of all parts of Christian India and applying them to seven fields in seven different sections of India's great expanse. The first is denominational and intensive; the second interdenominational and extensive. India has room for both and for many more of each. Both are built upon the principle of Indian initiative and employ Indian workers paid by Indian money.

In the early days of the N.M.S., its missionaries were all men, assisted perhaps by their wives, who with household cares could give only limited service. Later came the idea that here was a field for Indian women. At the last convention, the question of women's contribution and women's work was definitely raised, and Mrs. Appasamy took upon herself the burden of travel and appeal. Already she has organized contributing branches among the women of India's principal cities and is now anticipating a trip to distant Burmah for the same purpose. Rupees 8,000—about $2,300.00—lie in the treasury as the first year's response, much of it given in contributions of a few cents each from women in deep poverty, to whom such gifts are literally the "widow's mite."

The spending of the money is already planned. In the far north in a Punjabi village a house is now a building and its occupant is chosen. Miss Sirkar, a graduate now teaching in Kinnaird College, Lahore, has determined to leave her life within college walls, to move into the little house in the isolated village, and there on one third of her present salary to devote her trained abilities to the solution of rural problems. It is a new venture for an unmarried woman. It requires not only the gift of a dedicated life, but also the courage of an adventurous spirit. Elementary school teaching, social service, elementary medical help—these are some of the "jobs" that face this new missionary to her own people.

But, to return to Mrs. Appasamy, she not only organizes other people for work, but in the depressed communities of Madras herself carries on the tasks of social uplift. As supervisor of a Social Service organization, she has the charge of the work carried on in fifteen outcaste villages. With the aid of several co-workers frequent visits are made. Night schools are held for adults who must work during the hours of daylight, but who gather at night around the light of a smoky kerosene lantern to struggle with the intricacies of the Tamil alphabet. Ignorant women, naturally fearful of ulterior motives, are befriended, until trust takes the place of suspicion. The sick are induced to go to hospitals; learners are prepared for baptism; during epidemics the dead are buried. During the great strike in the cotton mills, financial aid was given. Hull House, Chicago, or a Madras Pariah Cheri—the stage setting shifts, but the fundamental problems of ignorance and poverty and disease are the same the world around. The same also is the spirit for service, whether it shines through the life of Jane Addams or of Mrs. Appasamy.

With the "Blue Triangle."

The autumn of 1906 saw the advent of the first Indian student at Mt. Holyoke College. Those were the days when Oriental students were still rare and the entrance of Dora Maya Das among seven hundred American college girls was a sensation to them as well as an event to her.

It is a far cry from the wide-spreading plains of the Punjab with their burning heats of summer to the cosy greenness of the Connecticut valley—a far cry in more senses than geographical distance. Dora had grown up in a truly Indian home, as one of thirteen children, her father a new convert to Christianity, her mother a second generation Christian. The Maya Das family were in close contact with a little circle of American missionaries. An American child was Dora's playmate and "intimate friend." In the absence of any nearby school, an American woman was her teacher, who opened for her the door of English reading, that door that has led so many Oriental students into a large country. Later came the desire for college education. To an application to enter among the men students of Forman Christian College at Lahore came the principal's reply that she might do so if she could persuade two other girls to join her. The two were sought for and found, and these three pioneers of women's education in the Punjab entered classes which no woman had invaded before.

[Illustration: BABY ON SCALES]

Then came the suggestion of an American college, and Dora started off on a voyage of discovery that must have been epoch-making in her life. It is, as I have said, a far cry from Lahore to South Hadley. It means not only physical acclimatization, but far more delicate adjustments of the mind and spirit. Many a missionary, going back and forth at intervals of five or seven years, could tell you of the periods of strain and stress that those migrations bring. How much more for a girl still in her teens! New conventions, new liberties, new reserves—it was young David going forth in Saul's untried armor. Of spiritual loneliness too, she could tell much, for to the Eastern girl, always untrammelled in her expression of religious emotion, our Western restraint is an incomprehensible thing. "I was lonely," says Miss Maya Das, "and then after a time I reacted to my environment and put on a reserve that was even greater than theirs."

So six years passed—one at Northfield, four at Mt. Holyoke, and one at the Y.W.C.A. Training School in New York. Girls of that generation at Mt. Holyoke will not forget their Indian fellow student who "starred" in Shakespearian roles and brought a new Oriental atmosphere to the pages of the college magazine. Six years, and then the return to India, and another period of adjustment scarcely less difficult than the first. That was in 1910, and the years since have seen Miss Maya Das in various capacities. First as lecturer, and then as acting principal of Kinnaird College at Lahore, she passed on to girls of her own Province something of Mt. Holyoke's gifts to her. Now in Calcutta, she is Associate National Secretary of the Y.W.C.A.

It was in Calcutta that I met Miss Maya Das, and that she left me with two outstanding impressions. The first is that of force and initiative unusual in an Indian woman. How much of this is due to her American education, how much to her far-northern home and ancestry, is difficult to say. Whatever the cause, one feels in her resource and executive ability. In that city of purdah women, she moves about with the freedom and dignity of a European and is received with respect and affection.

The second characteristic which strikes one is the fact that Miss Maya Das has remained Indian. One can name various Indian men and some women who have become so denationalized by foreign education that "home" is to them the land beyond the water, and understanding of their own people has lessened to the vanishing point. That Miss Maya Das is still essentially Indian is shown by such outward token as that of dropping her first name, which is English, and choosing to be known by her Indian name of Mohini, and also by adherence to distinctively Indian dress, even to the embroidered Panjabi slippers. What matters more is the inward habit of mind of which these are mere external expressions.

In a recent interview with Mr. Gandhi, Miss Maya Das told him that as a Christian she could not subscribe to the Non-Co-operation Movement, because of the racial hate and bitterness that it engenders; yet just because she was a Christian she could stand for all constructive movements for India in economic and social betterment. One of Mr. Gandhi's slogans is "a spinning wheel in every home," that India may revive its ancient arts and crafts and no longer be clothed by the machine looms of a distant country. Miss Maya Das told him that she had even anticipated him in this movement, for she and other Christian women of advanced education are following a regular course in spinning and weaving, with the purpose of passing on this skill through the Rural Department of the Y.W.C.A.

Another pet scheme of Miss Maya Das is the newly formed Social Service League of Calcutta. Into its membership has lately come the niece of a Chairman of the All-India Congress, deciding that the constructive forces of social reform are better to follow than the destructive programme of Non-Co-operation. Miss Maya Das longs to turn her abounding energy into efforts toward purdah parties and lectures for the shut-in women of the higher classes, believing that in this way the Association can both bring new interests into narrow lives, and can also gain the help and financial support of these bored women of wealth toward work among the poor.

One of Miss Maya Das's interests is a month's summer school for rural workers, a prolonged Indian Silver Bay, held at a temperature of 112 in the shade, during the month of May when all schools and colleges are closed for the hot weather vacation. Last year women came to it from distant places, women who had never been from home before, who had never seen a "movie," who had never entered a rowboat or an automobile. Miss Maya Das's stereopticon lectures carried these women in imagination to war scenes where women helped, to Hampton Institute, to Japan, and suggested practical ways of assisting in tuberculosis campaigns and child welfare. After four weeks of social enjoyment and Christian teaching they returned again to their scattered branches with the curtain total of their results from 88 in Newark to 355 in Madras.

[Illustration: PUTTING SPICES IN BABY'S MILK
Notice Feeding Vessels, Shell and Tin Cup]

What is Dr. Vera Singhe doing about it? With her two medical assistants, her corps of nurses, and the increasing number of health visitors whom she herself has trained, she has been able to reduce the death rate among the babies in her care during 1920 from the city rate of 280 for that year to 231.

But enough of statistics. More enlightening than printed reports is a visit to the Triplicane Health Centre, where in the midst of a congested district work is actually going on. We shall find no up-to-date building with modern equipment, but a middle-class Hindu house, adapted as well as may be to its new purpose. Among its obvious drawbacks, there is the one advantage, that patients feel themselves at home and realize that what the doctor does in those familiar surroundings they can carry over to their own home life.

Our visit happens to be on a Thursday afternoon, which is Mothers' Day. Thirty or more have gathered for an hour of sewing. It is interesting to see mothers of families taking their first lessons in hemming and overcasting,

Presently we fell into some casual talk, the inconsequent remarks common to chance acquaintance the world over. More intimate conversation followed, and before the end of the short journey together, I knew who Miss Paru was. The oldest daughter of a liberal Hindu lawyer on the Malabar Coast, she was performing the astounding feat of taking a medical course at the Men's Government College in Madras, while systematically breaking her caste by living at the Y.W.C.A. I almost gasped with astonishment. "But what do your relatives say?" I asked. "Oh," she replied, "my father is the head of his family and an influential man in our town. He does as he pleases and no one dares to object."

That was twelve years ago. Yesterday for the second time I met my traveling companion of long ago. She is now Dr. Paru, assistant to Dr. Kugler in the big Guntur Women's Hospital, with its hundred beds, managing alone its daily dispensary list of one hundred and fifty patients, and performing unaided such difficult major operations as a Caesarean section for a Brahman woman, of whom Dr. Kugler says, "The patient had made many visits to Hindu shrines, but the desire of her life, her child, was the result of an operation in a Mission Hospital. In our Hospital her living child was placed in her arms as a result of an operation performed by a Christian doctor."

How did Dr. Paru, the Hindu medical student, develop into Dr. Paru, the Christian physician? I asked her and she told me, and her answers were a series of pictures as vivid as her own personality.

First, there was Paru in her West Coast Home, among the cocoanut palms and pepper vines of Malabar where the mountains come down to meet the sea and the sea greets the mountains in abundant rains. Over that Western sea once came the strange craft of Vasco di Gama, herald of a new race of invaders from the unknown West. Over the same sea to-day come men of many tongues and races, and Arab and African Negroes jostle by still in the bazaars of West Coast towns. Such was the setting of Paru's home. During her childhood days certain visitors came to its door, Bible women with parts of the New Testament for sale, little paper-bound Gospels with covers of bright blue and red. The contents meant nothing to Paru then, but the colors were attractive, and for their sake she and her sister, childlike, bought, and after buying, because they were schoolgirls and the art of reading was new to them, read.

The best girls' school in that Malabar town was a Roman Catholic convent. It was there that Paru's education was given to her, and it was there that prayer, even in its cruder forms, entered into her experience. Religious teaching was not compulsory for non-Christian pupils, but, when the sisters and their Christian following gathered each morning for prayers, the doors were not shut and among other onlookers came Paru, morning after morning, drawn partly by curiosity, partly by a sense of being left out. Never in all her years in that school did the Hindu child join in the Christian service, but at home, when father and mother were not about, she gathered her sister and younger brothers into a corner and taught them in childish words to tell their wants and hopes and fears to the Father in Heaven.

The lawyer-father was the abiding influence in the daughter's growth of mind and soul. A liberal Hindu he would have been called. In reality, he was one of that unreckoned number, the Nicodemuses of India, who come to Jesus by night, who render Him unspoken homage, but never open confession. A man of broad religious interests, he read the Hindu Gita, the Koran, and the Gospels; and among them all the words of Jesus held pre-eminence in his love and in his life. When in later years he found his daughter puzzling over Bible commentaries to clear up some question of faith, he asked impatiently, "Why do you bother with those books? Read the words of Jesus in the Gospels and act accordingly. That is enough." Father and daughter were wonderful comrades. In all the years of separation when, as student and doctor, Paru was held on the opposite side of India, long weekly letters went back and forth, and events and thoughts were shared. When the hour of decision came, and the girl ventured into untried paths where the father could not follow, there were separation and misunderstanding for a time, but that time was short. The home visits were soon resumed and the Christian daughter was once more free to share home and meals with her Hindu family. And when one day the father said, "If a person feels a certain thing to be his duty, he should do it, whatever the cost," Paru rejoiced, for she knew that her forgiveness was sealed.

Dr. Paru's entrance into the world of medicine was due to her father's wish rather than her own. He was of that rare type of social reformer who acts more than he speaks. Believing that eventually his daughter would marry, he felt that as a doctor from her own home she could carry relief and healing into her small neighborhood. Paru, to please her father, went into the long grind of medical college, conquered her aversion for the dissecting table, and "made good." What does he think, one wonders, as, looking upon her to-day with the clearer vision of the life beyond, he sees the beloved daughter, thoughts of home and husband and children put aside, but with her name a household word among the women of a thousand homes. Ask her what she thinks of medicine as a woman's profession and her answer will leave no doubt whether she believes it worth while.

Actual decision for Christ was a thing of slow growth, its roots far back in memories of bright-covered Gospels and convent prayers, fruit of open confession maturing only during her years of service at Guntur. Life in the Madras Y.W.C.A. had much to do with it. There were Indian Christian girls, fellow students. "No," said Dr. Paru, "they didn't talk much about it; they had Christian ideals and tried to live them." There was a secretary, too, who entered into her life as a friend. "Paru," she said at last, "you are neither one thing nor the other. If you aren't going to be a Christian, go back and be a Hindu. At least, be something." At Guntur there were the experiences of Christian service and fellowship. Finally, there were words spoken at a Christian meeting, "words that seemed meant for me"; and then the great step was taken, and Dr. Paru entered into the liberty that has made her free to appear outwardly what she long had been at heart.

Such are a few of those Indian women whom one delights to honor. They broke through walls of custom and tradition and forced their way into the open places of life. Few they are and widely scattered, yet their influence is past telling.

To-day Lucknow, Madras, and Vellore are sending out each year their quota of educated women, ready to find their place in the world's work. It gives one pause, and the desire to look into the future—and dream. Ten years hence, twenty, fifty, one hundred! What can the dreamer and the prophet foretell? When those whom we now count by fives and tens are multiplied by the hundred, what will it mean for the future of India and the world? What of the gladness of America through whose hand, outstretched to share, there has come the release of these latent powers of India's womanhood?

But what of the powers not released? What of the "mute, inglorious" company of those who have had no chance to become articulate? There among the road-menders, going back and forth all day with a basket of crushed stone upon her head, toils a girl in whose hand God has hidden the cunning of the surgeon. No one suspects her powers, she least of all, and that undeveloped skill will die with her, undiscovered and unapplied. "To what purpose is this waste?"

Into your railway carriage comes the young wife of a rajah. Hidden by a canopy of crimson silk, she makes her aristocratic entrance concealed from the common gaze. Her life is spent within curtains. Yet she is the descendant of a Mughal ancestor who carried off and wedded a Rajput maiden. In her blood is the daring of Padmini, the executive power of Nur Jahan. With mind trained and exercised, she would be the administrative head of a woman's college. Again,—"To what purpose is this waste?"

Who dares to compute the sum total of lives wasted among the millions of India's women because undiscovered? Will American girls grudge their gifts to help in the discovery? Will American girls grudge the investment of their lives?

>   Only like souls I see the folk thereunder,
> Bound who should conquer, slaves who should be kings,
> Hearing their one hope with an empty wonder,
> Sadly contented with a show of things.
> Then with a rush the intolerable craving
> Shivers throughout me like a trumpet call;
> Oh, to save these! To perish for their saving,
> Die for their life, be offered for them all.

MYERS

THE END

www.ingramcontent.com/pod-product-compliance
Lightning Source LLC
Chambersburg PA
CBHW081116080526
44587CB00021B/3615